Capital Budgeting – The Investment And Financing Decision

SADANAND PUJARI

Published by SADANAND PUJARI, 2024.

Table of Contents

Copyright 1

About... 2

Introduction.. 3

Measure of Risk 8

Risk & Discount Rates 16

Simulation Models 20

Investment Impact on Portfolio...................................... 24

Standard Deviation, Variance, & Coefficient of Variation..... 29

Standard Deviation, Variance, & Coefficient of Variation..... 42

Expected Value, Standard Deviation, & Coefficient of Variation 51

Expected Value, Standard Deviation, & Coefficient of Variation 59

Coefficient of Variation Three Investment Alternatives 66

Coefficient of Variation & Investment Risk.............................. 74

Coefficient of variation Two Project Alternatives 79

Expected Value & Net Present Value Even Yearly Cash Flows.. 86

Expected Value & Coefficient of Variation Investment Options... 94

Expected Value in Capital Budgeting Decision Uneven Payments 101

Expected Value for Multiple Years & NPV 106

Standard Deviation, Variance, & Coefficient of Variation...117

Expected Value, Standard Deviation, & Coefficient of Variation 132

Expected Value, Standard Deviation, & Coefficient of Variation 141

Expected Value, Standard Deviation, & Coefficient of Variation 149

Coefficient of Variation Three Investment Alternatives 156

Coefficient of Variation & Investment Risk............................165

Expected Value & Net Present Value Even Yearly cash Flows..169

Expected Value & Coefficient of Variation Investment Options 176

Expected Value in Capital Budgeting Decision Uneven Payments 184

What Next...189

Copyright

Copyright © 2024 by **SADANAND PUJARI**

All rights reserved. No part of this book may be reproduced, scanned, or distributed in any printed or electronic form without permission. Please do not participate in or encourage piracy of copyrighted materials in violation of the author's rights. Purchase only authorized editions.

Capital Budgeting – The Investment And Financing Decision

Elements Of The Investment Decision And How To Finance The Investment

First Edition: Jun 2024

Book Design by **SADANAND PUJARI**

About

This Book will cover the use of risk assessment tools as they relate to capital budgeting and investment decisions and how to use them.

When making long term investment and capital budgeting decisions we need to consider the time value of money. The decision-making process will estimate future cash flows and then apply our time value of money concepts to those future cash flows.

This Book will take a step back in the process, providing tools to best estimate the future cash flows. To make the best decision we will need to estimate what the future cash flows will be and the likelihood of those cash flows, giving us numbers we can apply present value concepts to while also taking into consideration risk.

To help measure risk, the Book will use statistical tools including the population mean, population variance, standard deviation, and coefficient of variation.

We will provide a quick overview of these statistical concepts in general and then consider how we can apply them to measuring risk for investment and capital budgeting decisions.

Introduction

We're going to look into statistical types of tools to analyze the risk with relation to capital budgeting and investment decisions. Quick recap of the capital budgeting decisions. Those are those long term types of decisions usually involving us putting money down up front in order to get future returns. Those returns usually affect multiple periods in the future and therefore we need time value of money calculations typically to assess those types of decisions, those tools for the time value of money being the net present value calculation and the internal rate of return.

If you want more detail on those calculations, take a look at the prior chapter when we go to them in detail. You'll note, however, that when we think about these net present value and internal rate of return types of calculations, we have to assume that we have determined what the future cash flows will be so that we can do the present value calculation. Obviously, we're talking about something that's going to happen in the future. We don't know what the cash flows could be. All we can do is make our best guess. So now we want to think about how to make the best guess and possibly some projects we can assume to be more risky than other projects and the projects that are more risky.

How do we deal with that with regards to our decision making process? How do we compare one project that has more risk, but possibly a higher return versus another project that has less risk if we can only put our money into one or the other of them? So risk the variability of future outcomes from an investment. So we have an investment. We're projecting what's going to happen in the future. We're going to try to put our assessment on the risk, the likelihood of one outcome versus another outcome happening.

We don't know what's going to happen in the future, but we can clearly look at where we're at now and try to assess how risky one decision would be versus another and then tailor our decision making process to take that into consideration and measure uncertainty in the decision. When we think about the likelihood of something happening in the future, we can think about the average or what we expect the expected value to be and then the spread of the data. How likely is that expected value to be? And we can then plot out the likelihood that we do not think it's going to happen.

The more spread out the data, then the more risk that you would generally consider to be apparent. So, for example, if we look at this first option where we have three outcomes that we think possibly could happen, we're going to say A, B and C and possibly A's A thousand dollar return B, two thousand dollars and three three thousand dollars. B is going to be the one that we think is more likely to happen. We would call that kind of the average of the expected return with regards to our analysis. Then the question is, Will, how likely is it that B will actually take place? It's at fifty percent here and then we have twenty five for A and twenty five for C. This is a less spread out data set. Then we might see if we were having our analysis.

Look something like this where the mean or center point is at 30 percent and then we have more in the outer reaches here. This then would indicate in general that we have less likelihood that the mean or average will happen. We still believe the expected value will be at the center point, but there's a more spread out amount of data. Therefore, the likelihood of it not being at that center point increases. And that's going to generally increase risk, which is generally something that we would try to reduce. And Of course, down here, we now have the center point mean or average or the expected value at the twenty five percent.

Once again, risk has been spread out. There's more likelihood that it will not be at that center point, which increases the risk. Now note, when you look at actual data and we've run like motto's on this right here, we're looking at a bell shaped type of curve to see if the data points would fit into, you know, the standard deviations. We could start to talk about the standard deviations, how likely the point will be at the middle point. However, if you start looking at the actual data set and you see that it's skewed to the right, meaning, if the first one was going to be giving you a thousand dollars, two thousand dollars, three thousand dollars. Four thousand dollars, five thousand dollars, six thousand dollars, seven thousand dollars, the items to the right here would actually be away from the mean.

They would be an outcome that's not at the center point, but they would be beneficial. Right. Those would be added money as opposed to if the outcome was going to be on the left, then Of course, those would be less than what we would expect and that would be a bad a bad outcome. So generally, what we're going to take a look at is basically think about the data points, where is it going to fit in in a standard deviation type of analysis? And usually the more spread out the data, the worse it's going to be, because that's more likely that there's going to be. Risk, however, again, you want to look at the actual data points as well to consider, you know, what the spread of the actual data points would be and that could affect your decision making process as well.

So that's going to be the general process to start to talk about some of these statistical terms to organize our thoughts as we think about the future. Obviously, again, we don't know what's going to happen in the future. Everything that we're projecting into the future is projected, given it's something in the future. But this is a way that we can start to organize our thoughts so that we can make as best a decision as we can. So risk averse and the general rule for investments is usually making managerial decisions. We're going to be somewhat risk averse, meaning we're going to avoid risk unless expected return is high enough to make up for it. In other words, there's two things that we're typically considering with regards to our projects in the future. One is what we concentrated on in prior chapters, which is going to be the return. Is the return enough, the expected return that we think we're going to get enough to warrant the risk that we're taking on.

If we have a higher level of risk that's going to be happening, then we have to have an expected return. That's going to be enough to warrant the increase in the risk. And that leads us to believe basically as the risk level goes up, then people start to think that if the risk level is higher than the expected return is higher, that's not necessarily the case. As your expected return goes up, it's often the case that risk goes up. So when you're looking at projects that have a higher expected return, oftentimes there's going to be more risk involved in those particular points of projects. But it's quite possible to have risk go up without the expected return going up.

And those are typically the projects that we want to avoid, meaning the risk going up is not the thing that drives the expected return to go up necessarily. Risk can go up without the expected return going up. If the expected return is going up, then oftentimes that does come along with risk that will go up. And those are the areas that we need to basically focus on and decide is that risk going to be something that we want to take on with regards to the individual project? And we can also think about risk levels as they relate to us as a company as a whole as well. When we measure the risk involved with a particular type of project, does that fit well with our risk assessment? As we think about our whole holdings, our whole asset base, our whole investment portfolio?

Measure of Risk

We're thinking about risk as it relates to our capital budgeting and investment type decisions. Those investment decisions that are going to have an impact multiple periods into the future and risk is going to be measuring the uncertainty. So what's the variable of future outcome from an investment measures uncertainty in the investment. So the general rule, as we discussed in prior chapters, is that two components we're looking at are expected return and risk. Obviously, we want our expected return to be as high as possible.

And in general, we would like the risk to be as low as possible in the event where we're measuring projects, where the risk is going up and the return is going up, then we want to be able to consider whether or not the added return warrants the added risk. So the statistical tools that will take a look at and the best way to practice these statistical tools is to work through practice problems. We will have many practice problems to work with. They will be the statistical concepts of the population mean. This can also be called basically the average or the expected value. These are going to be the terms that you might see for, in essence, the mean calculation.

And notice, when you think about these calculations, oftentimes you think about them as we start off in statistics, learning them with a series of numbers, a data set of numbers, and then work and apply them to a little bit different of a structure here. And the population mean will basically be the expected value. When we think about them with our future component of analysis, we will talk about that more in our practice problems, the transition from basically analyzing just a list of numbers, possibly where you first saw some of these terms and then applying them to our future decision making process. And Of course, there's a lot more analysis, great material out there for mathematical concepts, statistical analysis and so on, that you can look up on YouTube or the Internet with your favorite browser.

We didn't have the population variance, which will be this calculation. We'll talk more about the calculations as we go through the practice problems. We just want to list them out. For now. We have the standard deviation and then we have the coefficient of variation. Now, note, for our purposes, as we're projecting into the future, we're oftentimes going to be looking at the mean, basically the average, because that's going to be, in essence, the expected value. In other words, if we have multiple things that we think can happen, we've run multiple projections into the future, then typically we take the average. The mean one averaged the expected value and thought that that's going to be what we expect to happen.

Then we want to think about what's going to be the variance from the mean, what's the spread from the mean, because that's going to help us with the determination as to the risk that will be involved. Now, the calculations for that from a statistical analysis could include the population variance and the standard variance of the standard deviation. But oftentimes when we're thinking about capital projects into the future, they have different investment amounts. Therefore, we'll be concentrating on the coefficient of variation to help us to measure the risk. So the two terms we're typically going to be looking at with regards to the two questions, we have one expected value that's going to be our average, the expected value, the mean in essence, of what we believe the expected outcomes could be, and then the coefficient of variation, which is going to be helping us to determine the level of risk.

Now, Of course, to get to the bottom line number, the coefficient of variation, we're going to need to calculate the standard deviation to get there near the standard deviation. And you need to calculate the population variance to get to the standard deviation. From a statistical point of view, Of course, the better you understand about all the concepts and how they're going to be related to each other, the better you are. So if you want to go from a mathematical standpoint, just in terms of the analysis of data, then again, a lot of material you can look up on that. So if we have our three different scenarios, once again, let's say this is scenario one, A, B, C and D, and we're going to say that A, B, C and D represent different values that we expect could happen in the future.

So we could have then we have a, B and one thousand B being the two thousand return, three C being the three thousand return. In this case, we would say that B would be our expected value, basically the average in this case. So we're going to say this is going to be our expected value. The question then is going to be how likely is the data set to be lying outside the expected value? Now, note, this gets a little confusing because we're not talking about a data set that basically already happened or analyzing a big population. We're trying to use these concepts to analyze the future, what we're going to think in the future. So the more spread out the data is from the the mean the concept is meaning this data set is more spread out from the center point has more likelihood that a point that lands in here will be somewhere outside the the middle point.

Then in this chart and this chart, it's going to be more spread out, so the general rule is the likelihood of the data that's going to be spread out more from the center point is going to give us more risk. Now, the typical kind of calculation for that would be the standard deviation. So the standard deviation would help us to say, OK, here's the data points that we expect to be happening. How likely are they going to be falling into a certain chapter if we were to graph them as basically a bell curve? Right. That's going to be the concept of it. And the more likely, you know, so that would mean the greater the standard deviation that we have, the more there is variance.

And that would be an indication that you have more risk. Now, the problem with the standard deviation is that we could be dealing with projects that have different expected values. So in other words, if this middle term here, the average is different, which it well could be, given the fact that when we're talking about capital projects, we could be comparing projects that are completely different in nature and the level of years that could be involved could be different and a whole bunch of components could be different. So if we have two projects that have different values for the expected value, this first one, for example, having 5000 standard deviation of 400, then compared to this one, that has an expected value of only 500, which is the center point, in essence, the average of the mean.

In essence, the standard deviation is going to be 150. Notice this one has a less standard deviation than this one would, which would lead you to believe that this one then, if you were just to look at the standard deviation, would have less risk. But that's not generally the case here, because this one has a much higher expected value. And you could see that from just the graphical re chapter that it looks like the data is going to be more centered towards the middle, which means that you would think it would have less risk or this one is going to have more data. It looks like it's towards the tails, which means that you would think that it would have more risk.

And that, Of course, is the result of the relationship between the standard deviation calculation in dollars as compared to the expected value or basically the average here versus here. So this number doesn't tell us as much by itself when comparing once again, different projects that have different expected value. The solution to that then is to use the coefficient of variation which is going to take that standard deviation and divide it by the mean or the average or the expected value. In essence, you can basically think of those three terms as kind of like the same thing when you're jumping back and forth from statistics. Statistics is going to call it the mean in the average person on the street. I'm going to call it the average. You know, Excel is going to call it the average. And here we're basically calling it an expected value.

So for the most part, you can pretty much switch those out. So then if this one will be used to remove the problem caused by the different investment sizes. So now once we do this calculation, we'll come up with a term which by itself wouldn't tell us too much about the data. But when compared to another project, such as these two projects could then give us a comparison to help us to see the spread of the data in a relative way. And that could help us with our calculation of risk. So those are going to be the standard. Two terms we'll look at are going to be the expected value, and then we're not going to spend a lot of time on the standard deviation due to the fact that we're measuring things of different sizes typically.

And we'll jump on over to the coefficient of variation generally. So the best way to get an idea that is just to work on practice problems will be to do a lot of practice problems. So then we have the EBITA, the risk measure commonly used with relation to the portfolio of common stocks. When we're thinking about common stock, we can use other kinds of methods because we have indexes in the market to help us out with that. We're not going to spend as much time here because we're focusing on those capital projects oftentimes and using these tools for the capital projects where we don't have the benefit of the indexes. So it measures volatility of returns on individual stock relative to the returns on the stock market index. Then we have the capital budgeting factors.

So we have the expected return and the risk. So remember, whenever you're thinking about these decisions, investment decisions in general and Of course with these capital budgeting decisions as a type of investment decision, these are the two things that we are waiting for. Also note that the larger the decision is, then the more important it is to get the balance right the first time. In other words, if you're investing in something that's a short term investment, then and like stocks and you're trading stocks and you could trade them around from period to period, then you have some leeway to try to test things out, see if it worked and then test it out again. You can do trial and error. You can tinker with something. But these capital budgeting decisions, remember, are different in nature that you can't tinker with a capital budgeting decision because if you're buying.

A whole nother property. If you're buying a whole factory in order to or doing a large merger or something like that, or buying a big piece of equipment, just like on the personal side, buying a new car or something, that thing is going to last you for some time. So it's not like you can say, you know, I tried this decision and I will try something else tomorrow and see if it works out better or worse. There's some types of decisions that you just don't have that option and those types of decisions you have to basically what they call measure twice, cut once, just like if you're measuring the doorframe, you don't want to cut the piece of wood to short the first time because you can't redo it there. You gotta go buy a new piece of wood.

So with these capital budgeting decisions, because they're long term decisions, we want to, Of course, spend more time to get this measure right. Then we might do it on a normal day to day like managerial type of decisions. Obviously, the expected return. We want to maximize the expected return if we can. We want to minimize the risk, which generally means we want to minimize the variance that could be from the expected value that we would take. Generally, that means that note that if the expected return goes up, oftentimes expected return goes up and it includes a higher level of risk. That's typically the case.

But remember, the fact that risk goes up, the risk going up is not the thing that is holding up.

The expected return risk could go up. An expected return may not. And those are the things we want to weed out if expected. Expected return goes up on a particular project. It's likely that risk will go up, but it's also likely that risk can easily go up without expected return going up. So in a situation where the expected, expected return does not go up and risk goes up, then Of course we want to pick the project that's going to have the better expected return and the lower risk in the situation. Our expected return goes up and risk goes up. Then we have to measure whether or not the risk that is going up is worth it with regards to the return that we're going to possibly get, the higher expected return. And we can measure that on an individual investment standpoint as well as how it fits in our overall company structure, our investment portfolio, in essence, to mitigate risk on that level.

Risk & Discount Rates

We're continuing to talk about risk as it relates to capital budgeting, investment type of decisions, those investment types of decisions that typically will involve a large outflow up front and then an impact of inflows multiple years into the future. Two components to the decisions, major, two categories that help us for the thought process, that being what's our expected return for the capital project and then the level of risk. Now, we focused a lot on, once we know the expected return using our present value tools, that being the net present value and the internal rate of return calculations to then figure out and think about one project versus another or whether or not a project would be worth taking on.

For more information about that, take a look at a prior chapter. We're now thinking about the risk component and putting that into practice. How can we apply the risk component? So we've looked at some statistical data now. We've looked at the idea of applying statistical concepts to get an idea about the risk, the risk from one project to another. And again, for practice. With that, the best way to understand these problems is to run through example problems. We do have many example problems, but now the question is, once I know what the risk is, what do I do with that with regards to my calculation process? How do I fit it into my decision process? In other words, if I know one project has a higher risk than the other and I can only basically pick one project versus the other, how do I take that risk into consideration with my assessment when my normal tools for a capital project are the net present value calculation and the internal rate of return.

So different capital projects will need different discount rates if they have different risk levels. So answer being, we can change the discount rates, we can adjust the discount rates as the risk levels will change. So if we have two projects that are going to be in place, then one project we determined to be more risky than the other project. When we apply our net present value calculation and the internal rate of return, we might then adjust or increase the discount rate for the project that includes more risk within it. So if the risk level is average, the standard cost of capital discount rate is used. So if we have an average project, it's an average amount of risk, a standard amount of risk. We might calculate our weighted average cost of capital use, our standard cost of capital discount rate as our normal required rate of return.

That in essence being the floor discount rate, the discount rate that we would have to clear the discount rate at which if we calculated the net present value, the net present value would have to be over zero in order for us to accept the project, as we discussed in prior chapters, given the fact that we would then have cleared that discount rate, if the risk is above average, the discount rate used will be higher than the cost of capital. So if we're then looking at a project that has a discount, that has a risk level higher than the normal risk level, then we're going to compensate with that by then increasing the discount rate. And if that discount rate is basically our hurdle rate for that particular project, then we'd need the project to clear that discount rate in order for us to basically accept the project.

And we can use that for our comparison purposes. So the risk level is generally measured by the coefficient of variation. So remember what we talked about, that last chapter in our kind of statistical concepts? The best way to get an idea about the spread of data is to do practice problems. We will work on many practice problems so risk related to long term projects. The longer the project, the more difficult the forecasting. Obviously, when you're looking at the future further out into the future, there's a whole lot more uncertainty and unknowns. Then if we look shorter into the future to compensate for that, we could increase discount rates used for late cash flows due to increased uncertainty. So one method you might put into place is you could get a little bit more complex on a capital budgeting project.

We've seen these capital budgeting projects that could get quite complex with regards to the cash flows that might happen in the future. We might do an entire budgeting analysis to determine what the cash flows would be. We might have different cash flows from year to year in the future, which we can then present value with the use of our net present value calculations. But we also might say, hey, the risk is different from year to year. Year one might have less risk than a year or two and so on. So we could apply then. Different discount rates apply to different years. And as you can imagine, how when using the net present value calculation, we can basically use different discount rates for the returns. And that's another method that might be applied.

So you might see tables, something like this. Then when you're calculating your risk and you're then trying to apply that to a capital project, you might say, well, the risk is low. Then we're going to use the five per. Maybe that's our cost of capital, maybe that's the floor risk that we would need to clear a normally moderate seven percent average that is nine percent above average and in high risk, 15 percent very high at 18 percent. So now we're saying, hey, look, if you got a project that's pretty, pretty low on the risk level and we have the money to put into that project, then we want to clear the five percent, possibly that being the cost of capital. If, on the other hand, you have a high project with a higher amount of risk, we might say, hey, look, that, you know, the expected return is good on that.

We like the expected return or possibly. But we want to do our calculation based on the fact that there's a whole lot more risk. And so if we did apply our net present value types of calculation, given the higher risk levels, then they would have to clear a higher threshold for that net present value calculation in order for it to be acceptable. So you could see how we can then take the risk that we would calculate and then say, OK, well, how do I put this into comparison in practice so I can compare and make decisions on whether to take a capital budgeting project or compare different capital budgeting projects. One way we might see that applied is to adjust the discount rates as we apply them to the capital budgeting process and the calculations of the net present value of them.

Simulation Models

Time to take your chance with corporate finance simulation models can help with forecasting or predicting outcomes of capital budgeting decisions, the capital budgeting decisions being those longer term types of decisions, the typical outline of them having an outflow up front. And then we expect future inflows from that initial investment, that initial outflow, because it's going to have an impact on multiple periods into the future and because it's usually substantial in dollar amount, we spend more time in order to make the decision making process for these items, the primary tools that we use, net present value calculation and internal rate of return. Now because we're looking out into the future and there's a lot of unknowns in the future.

Modeling methods can help us to kind of take a better picture of those types of unknowns by running multiple variations. So the use of computers allows the running of numerous variations. A Monte Carlo model will use random variables for inputs. So note, when we're thinking about the future cash flows, we're going to talk about, well, how can we know what the future cash flows can be? Because I have to predict the future cash flows in order to then run our net present value calculations and possibly the internal rate of return calculations. But I don't really know what the future cash flows will be. And that's kind of what we're talking about here. More of the unknowns in the future and the risk that could be involved in the future.

So you can imagine with these longer term types of modeling that there could be a lot of things where we're saying, hey, there could be a range. We think the outcomes might be within this range and there could be some degree of randomness that we just don't know about. And we would like to run a model in order to show that degree of randomness. And with the computer methods now, we can apply that degree of randomness to some areas in our models. And we might say, you know, this particular part of the calculation, we want you to put in some random numbers between these intervals and then the generator can give you results and plot what the results will be, just randomly picking some of these components.

And you can see that obviously, if you have multiple random variables, these models can get quite complex. It would be very difficult to do them mathematically because it gets quite complex once you have a few different models. So you can think of it. We've been using the to a goal seek and Excel, which basically backs into a number and algebraic number when you have one unknown without doing the algebra, just kind of forces it by randomly picking numbers until it gets the right one. You can kind of think about that as what you're trying to do with a Monte Carlo type of method or with these modeling methods. It's to say, hey, I want you to give me the outcomes and have this random set right here and then just pick random numbers that are within the conditions that we set and we'll just see what outcomes we get and those outcomes we get.

We can actually kind of plot the outcomes. And hopefully that'll give us a better picture of the probabilities of what could happen in the future and a better idea of what the actual risk is. So repetition of the same random process many times helps with the decision making. So simulation models allow us to test different combinations of events. So obviously when we run these different models, we can run different, different ideas of what's going to happen into the future. Different sets of events can be used to test possible changes in variable conditions, and can generate probability acceptance curves to help with capital budgeting decisions. So if we set basically, you know, outcomes to come out of the model, we can basically plot those outcomes and then come up with a curve on those outcomes. And that could help us with our modeling decision process as well.

Allow us to ask multiple what if questions. And this is really important because that's really what you're doing when you're forecasting into the future. You're trying, you're trying to come in to say, you know, how likely is this going to happen? What if this happened? Obviously, there's an infinite number of what-if questions that could come into play when you're making a capital budgeting decision that's going to have an impact five or ten years into the future. So you want to ask the major questions and then try to figure out which ones are going to be the most relevant to your decision making process, then try to look at the likelihood of those events happening and what's the best case scenario.

The worst case scenario? What if multiple of these things went bad at the same time? What's the likelihood of multiple of these? What if analysis is going bad, some of these big factors versus going good and so on. And you can then put these into the model. And again, with computer models like you have the same kind of idea that we're talking about here when we go through the process into your general thought process. But Of course, with the computer models, you can again set those kinds of ranges and you can allow some Rande. Variables to basically then be generated and let the computer do what it does and give you the outcomes based on a random generation of variables, and that could be useful.

Investment Impact on Portfolio

We've been thinking here about longer term type of investments, capital project type of investments, those that typically are characterized as having an outflow up front that will be resulting in, hopefully, future inflows multiple years into the future, although these are longer term type of difficult decisions, oftentimes in some shorter type of investment decisions, we do have similar characteristics to normal investment decisions you may hear about with personal type of investments, investing for your personal savings, stocks, bonds and so on, as well as shorter term type of investments for the business side of things as well.

The things that you typically would hear were things like diversify your portfolio so that you can mitigate the risk. Those things apply to the longer term type of investments as well. It's just that, Of course, when we think about the longer term type of investments, we also have to take into consideration the added risk involved in the fact that we can't just flip and change our decision quite as easily with a shorter term type of investment. So whether you're thinking about investments or like managerial type of decisions in general, whenever you're looking at the short term things that you can change, then you have that component where you can do the tinkering type of thing. You could test things out if there's not a lot of consequence to the decision that you're making at that point in time. But multiple decisions will have consequences. You can test things out and try things and see what happens.

Longer term type of decisions. Of course, you can't, you know, just, you know, stop the project that you just went into. That was a 10 year project quite as easily. You might be able to if you decide that it's no longer profitable. But that's going to be a much more difficult decision to take into place. However, when you're thinking about the decision in general with regards to your overall type of investment decisions, we want to assess the risk for that individual decision. And then, Of course, we also want to take that decision and see how it fits into our overall investment strategy as well. So investments that are highly correlated will not provide diversification against risk.

So clearly, just like with a portfolio, the idea is diversification, oftentimes, because that's going to be lowering the risk. So if something that's going to be correlated, then that means if you have, for example, investments where if one goes up, the other one goes up, they're linked together, or the things that are going to cause them to go up are the same things. So if you have, for example, all one kind of stocks in your stock portfolio and they all go up when the economy is in one certain condition and then they all go down when something else happens, then that's not good for. Stocks are too correlated and they'll look super. Your stock portfolio then will look really good if all those things that happened to make your entire investment portfolio happen to be good. But if they happen to be bad, then your portfolio will go down quite quickly.

And that's why oftentimes you think about stocks and bonds, which are supposed to be somewhat different in their correlation to give you some hedge against basically problems so that everything's not going the same way. So conversely, investments that are negatively correlated will provide greater risk reduction. So obviously, when you take on the risk reduction with negatively correlated items, then you're not going to basically admit that you don't know exactly what's going to happen in the future. Right. If I knew exactly what's going to happen in the future, I can put all my stuff in one area and take full advantage and maximize, you know, everything being correlated the same way towards whatever is going to happen.

But we don't know what's going to happen. So we have to basically hedge against risk. That could happen in the future. And that's really the art of investment over the long term is being able to say, hey, look, I really don't know what's going to happen. And I'm going to basically often and I'm and I'm going to basically set up my portfolio so that I can mitigate my risk so that negatively correlated correlations will basically help with that. And that's generally the stocks and bonds having some weighted weighting between them. When you're talking about normal investments, when you're talking about long term capital projects, you have a similar type of thing. If you invest in a lot of long term capital projects and things turn out the way you think they're going to turn out, you will look like a superstar. But if things do not turn out the way you think they will, you'll look, you'll look horrible and, you know, it'll be all over.

You know, they could, you know, everything will be gone at that point in time. So that's why you want to basically hedge against it generally. And you could see this stuff kind of playing out all the time where people, you know, people make big bets and they can if someone's winning for a short period of time, it could just be luck, you know, that they that they that they have everything in the right spot at one time, but over. The long run, yeah, it may not turn out so well because you would think that nobody can predict the future for that long amount of time. So you need the diversification to really to really play it right. So investments that are uncorrelated provide moderate risk reduction.

So if they're not correlated at all, you know, then they're going to have some moderate risk reduction. They're not linked together. They're not going up for the exact same reasons or ones not making the other one go up or conversely, but they're not linked. So that, again, could give you some moderate level of risk assessment or reduction in risk level for the portfolio in total. So the extent of correlation among various capital projects and investment. So then you can get into trouble trying to calculate exactly what the correlation is and you can get more technical on, you know, what do we think the correlation is for any particular decision? Values between negative one and one could be used for our correlation. Negative correlations possibly being more closer to point, negative point to and for that would be negative correlation.

So negative correlations possibly being closer to like negative point two and positive correlations around, you know, positive point three. So risk reduction combining risky assets with low risk or negatively correlated assets can lower the risk. So that's obviously going to be our objective here. We want to get the risk level to where we think it's a manageable amount of a risk level balancing out, Of course, the risk and the potential reward. So obviously, what we're trying to do, the primary objective, we want the highest return possible given the risk level. So we have that qualifier right. When we think about the highest return, we're thinking about the expected return normally and we're thinking about a long term capital project. We want the highest return with the qualifier given the risk level. Right.

And then we want the lowest risk level given the return level. So we're always doing that balancing act when we're thinking about new capital projects. What's going to be the level of the return that we expect to be happening? And all we can do is calculate kind of an expected return, because that's going to be, you know, the probability of what we think is going to be happen in the future and then tack on to that what we think the the risk level will be and balance out the risk level versus the return, noting that we have to consider the risk level for both the project in and of itself, as well as the project as it fits into our overall portfolio.

Standard Deviation, Variance, & Coefficient of Variation

We have our information up top going through some calculations down below. This chapter will be on statistical types of tools and concepts of a more mathematical type of chapter that will then use these tools and then use them in projections and whatnot in future chapters. So this is focused more on math to remind us about math related to basically a series of numbers and B. In math, there's a lot of great information on mathematical concepts such as these standard deviation variance and coefficient of variation. So you can search them on Google or any kind of whatever browser you want or YouTube, and you could probably find a lot of good information on it.

We're basically looking at a data set, a set of numbers and trying to get an idea about that set of numbers, a set of numbers possibly being a full population, the numbers representing a population of something, or they could be representing a sample of something we're typically going to use for population type of calculations here. And note, when you're thinking about statistics, then a lot of people are really skeptical about statistics because they hear the idea that basically people can lie with statistics. And that's true. People can lie with statistics, but people can lie with anything. Right. What people usually do when they lie with statistics, just like when they lie with anything, is they pull one piece of truth and then they build a bunch of lies around that one piece of truth that's basically holding up the whole thing of lies. Right.

And you can do that with one piece of truth and a verbal argument and whatnot as well. And statistics is vulnerable to that as well. But if you're doing statistics honestly, then what you're really trying to do is not get one piece of data. You want to analyze the population size with multiple pieces of data so that you can get a better idea of what the actual data set is saying. And that's kind of the idea of looking at statistics. Oftentimes when you're trying to figure out what the data set actually means, you'd like to take a look at different views, break it out in different ways, at different perspectives, at the data so you can see what it is representing, you know, in reality. So some of the concepts will take a look at if the population means the average of the population data points.

So the mean, remember, is basically the average, the average where you're going to sum up the population data points and then divide them by the population, which are the number of items that you're summing up. So that's going to be the could be called the mean or it could be called the average could and don't get that mixed up with a median, which is kind of like that center numbers. So that's usually kind of one of our starting calculations. When we're looking at a series of numbers, then we want to take a look at the variance, which is the dispersion of a set of data points around the mean. So that looks like a formula such as this population variance is going to be each data point minus the mean and then we're going to square it divided by the population size.

Again, the variance is going to be a concept that'll give us an idea of how much spread there is around the mean. So if you think about the mean, the average, then the next thing we want to look at is how clustered are the sets of data points around the average. So, for example, obviously, if you take each data point here minus the mean, the closer the data point is to the mean, then the smaller the number you're going to have here and then we're going to square it. So that'll be the concept of this. And then we'll move from there with the population variance. But that's the general concept that we want. Right.

We'll take the average, which is kind of like the middle. It's not the median, but it's the average. It's the meaning. And then we want to think about the variance, the variance being how dispersed are the data around that center point, which we have as the average. So to look at this, let's take a set of data points and we'll just count from one to five. Let's start out counting from one to five and do some of our analysis just based on that series of numbers. We have this series of numbers it could populate. It could represent some population of something. Our typical type of calculation with it would be possible to total it up to fifteen. If we divide that by the population size, which is one, two, three, four or five.

There's five of them, Of course, and that would give us the mean or average. So the fifteen are divided by five. Would be the three that would probably be our starting point when we're trying to analyze a set of numbers. Now, if we want to think about the population variance, then we could do something like this. We can use this calculation here, taking each of the numbers in the set, minus the mean squared over the population, which if we did that mathematically, would look like this one minus three, the mean. So that's the one minus the three down here, plus two, minus three to minus three squared, plus three, minus three three minus the mean three squared plus four minus three squared four minus four three squared and then five minus three squared divided by the population which is five, one, two, three, four or five in the population.

And that would give us the variance. If you do this like an Excel type of calculation, it would typically look something like this. We could set up our numbers here. We can take the mean, which is three. So we're taking each number in our data set. Then we're taking three that mean and we're going to compare them out. One, this is this part of it, Of course, one minus three, two minus three, three minus three. So if we take the difference, then we've basically done the whole, you know, numerator without squaring it. So now we're going to square each one of them and we've got these differences that we're going to square. Also note, when we have these differences here, some of them are negative, some of them are positive. And because these are distances from the mean, which is kind of like you're imagining the center point of this whole thing, they need to be positive.

So one way to get them to be positive is to square them. So squaring them will both make them positive and amplify the results. So if we square them, you pull out a trusty calculator. Remember, if you do this in a book problem, you need a calculator that can handle the square in. This one has a square button here. So you could say the two squared. So that's going to be the four here. But I think if you have anything other than squaring, you might have to use a different calculator which in the Windows calculator might be a scientific one, which you can get to by going to this little dropdown scientific calculator. And then you could take in the same two. And I'm going to say negative two, let's take the next two and then negative. And then you can go to the X, to the Y, X to the Y, and then we're going to take it to two.

And then there it goes. And it turns out to be, Of course, the positive four. That's going to be one of the functions of squaring it. So I'm going to go through here. If you did the same thing here, squaring the one, you're going to get one negative, one positive one zero is zero and then positive one is one X squared and then positive two is two if squared. So that's basically our numerator up top. Once we have that, then we can take a look at the we could sum them up and that's our numerator adding this up the four plus the one plus one plus the four. There's ten. Then we divide by which is five. The population one, two, three, four or five of them in the data set. So the ten divided by five is going to give us two. That being the population variance, the population variance. Now the population variance is squared, right. We still have this kind of squared component in it.

So it's often useful then to take that population variance and take the square root of it. So if we take that population variance of two and then square root, we get the one point four one four two one about so that. So that's going to be then the standard deviation. So that's what's going to be called the standard deviation. And then if we take the mean and we take that number, the one point four. So on divided by the average or mean divided by three, we're going to get then the point four, seven, one and so on and about point four seven, which is going to be the coefficient of variation. This might be represented in a percent or in a decimal.

So this number is going to be useful for us typically when we're measuring two different data sets and it'll become more clear as we go down and we see those two different data sets. So, again, normally you get the mean and then you're basically calculating the population variance to get an idea of the range around the mean. Taking the standard deviation then removes the squared component that you had up top, the squared component kind of amplifies the number, as well as removing the negative values, which gives us then the standard deviation. And then oftentimes we want to basically take the coefficient of variation because that'll help us to compare two different basic data sets of numbers and that'll become more apparent in the next. chapter also note that you could not do the next chapter, our next example problem down here, we will do a comparison so you could do these in Excel as well.

And we do this in Excel so you can see it there. So oftentimes when you see this in an Excel worksheet, you'll see it just mapped out and using the Excel calculations to calculate this note that it's often useful to actually map out the numbers this way, because mapping this out in Excel actually gives you an idea of what the what the numbers look like. You could see it like this difference column, having the negative and positive numbers that in and of itself gives you a pictorial view of the numbers of what's actually happening with the numbers. So it actually gives you more information to map this thing out in this format and see the numbers pictorially in that way.

And that can help you to visualize what the dataset actually means. So if we go down below, we could take the mean or average. And in Excel that would be the formula that equals the average. And then you take the sum of the data, which would be these five numbers, some of the five numbers that would give us three, the average, Of course, being adding up those five numbers divided by the number of units, which was five. And then we can take the standard deviation. That's going to be the S-T divi DCPI. Now, there's a dopy formula and there's a formula which can be slightly different, whether you're taking the population or the sample.

We're going to be working with population calculations here. If you're interested in the difference between the population and standard and sample, then you can there's a lot of a lot of information about that. If you research it on your favorite browser search or a YouTube search or something like that. And then we're going to take the variance. So you could do that with a formula which would be equal to Vaisakhi. Once again, there's a difference between P standard for population and S, which would stand for the sample and then take the range of the data and notice the range of the data is all the same here, which is our dataset one through five. And that gave us our two, Of course.

And then we got the coefficient of variation, which would be the same calculation, the same format that we did up top, that took the standard deviation over the mean standard deviation divided by the mean. So you could basically represent your data pretty quickly with the use of Excel formulas if you had access to Excel. But remember, Of course, we want to understand what is actually happening so that we see the numbers say something to us. So they actually mean something for us so we can analyze the data. Now, if we have two data sets, let's take these two data sets. First one, one, two, three, three, five, six, seven, eight, nine, 11. So it's not just one through 11. We got a couple of repeating threes here and it skips 10 to 11. And then the second data sets 20, 40, 60, 60, 100, 120, 140, 160, 180 and 220.

And so what we want to do is compare these two data sets with our analysis here. Now, there should be some similarities with these two data sets. So we would like our analysis to kind of give us a pictorial rechapter of them to kind of see what those similarities are. And you might see it here. The pattern is basically this: this dataset is just 20 or the data set one times twenty. One times twenty is twenty two times twenty four to three times twenty six to three times 2060 and so on. So notice these data sets, if they were represented in dollars for example, or are representing different dollar amounts.

But the variance around basically the mean has something in common there that are exactly the same in the disbursement in a sense. And we'd like to capture that in our analysis when we're thinking about our data analysis. So let's put let's breakdown our data analysis down here and we'll do the same kind of thing. And so note, we're taking basically this formula now, the population. Hold on a second. The population variance, so we'll take our data, then let's pick up our data. This is the first series of numbers here, and then we'll pick up the mean, which I'm going to just simply calculate the mean for us. Now, the mean calculation, if we were to do this with a trusty calculator, take me a little second here.

It's going to be one plus two plus three plus three plus five plus six plus plus eight plus nine plus one. And divide that by I think there's 10. Right. One, two, three, four, five, six, seven, eight, nine, ten. Divided by ten means or average is 5.5. So we're going to take our data set and subtract minus the mean or average 5.5. So one minus five point five is four point five, two minus five point five is the negative three point five, three minus five point five is a negative 2.5 five 5.5 three minus five point five negative two point five five minus five point five. Negative point five six minus five point five point five seven minus five point five, one point five eight minus five point five, two point five and nine minus 5.5 three point five eleven minus five point five 5.5.

So now we took our differences here and now we'll square them. So that's basically our numerator. We're going to square them now. So if I take the 4.5 and square, I'll just do one of them in the trusty calculator here. So if we do the trusty calculator and just take the 4.5 and squared, we get the twenty point twenty five, twenty point twenty five gets rid of the negative and amplifies it. So the three point five squared is twelve point twenty five, 2.5 squared is six point twenty five. Two point five squared is a two point twenty five. The point five squared is to point to five. Obviously, these ones closer to the mean that you can see here and squaring them, you know, then we'll square them, removing the negative side and amplifying them. So we got the point.

Five is the point twenty five, the one point five, the two point twenty five, the two point five to six point twenty five and so on. So then if we add these up, the total on the squared items, if I add up, this column is going to be the ninety six fifty, ninety six fifty population size, just counting them. One, two, three, four, five, six, seven, eight, nine, ten of them. So the ninety six point five divided by the ten is the population variance, the nine point sixty five. But note again, this variance has kind of like those squared numbers in them. So although this gives us a variance, if we're talking dollars here, they'd be talking like square dollars.

So we want to now kind of remove the squared component from the population. Variance would give us the standard deviation, the three point one one, which if they were in dollars, would be like dollar units. But then we might want to divide by the mean 5.5. So three point one one divided by the 5.5 gives us the coefficient of variation. This number is not too useful for us unless we're comparing it to another set of data because it gives us basically an idea of one set versus the other. So let's take a look at the second set here, the second set of numbers, the 20 to 40 and so on, the same set as here. The mean then if we calculate the main, let's do that. That'll be fun. Let's just do it.

Twenty plus forty plus 60 plus 60 plus 100 plus 120 plus 140 plus 160 plus 180 plus two two zero divided by the number of units, ten of them if I count them out, divided by ten. So dividing by ten is going to give us the one ten. So that's going to be the average all the way down one ten. And then we'll take the difference between these and notice as we take the difference. I will start to see some similarity between these two numbers because of the similarity and disbursement. Right. So we got the one the twenty minutes to one ten is ninety and negative. Ninety to 40 minus the one 110 is negative seventy sixty minus one ten is negative fifty sixty not minus one.

Ten is negative fifty. You could see kind of a parallel trend here that's happening. And then one hundred minus one ten is ten. The one twenty minus one ten is ten. So you could see a similar trend happening as we, as we go through these differences. The 140 miles to 110 is thirty. 160 minus one ten is fifty. The one eighty minus one ten is seventy and then the one twenty minus one ten is one ten. Now if we square these then we're going to take them all and square them. I'll just do one of them. So if we took that ninety for example, ninety are negative and it would be a negative ninety and squared it squared. It's going to be one eight one zero zero. So we got the one I'm sorry, the eight one zero zero seventy square four nine zero zero fifty square two five zero zero.

Fifty square negative, 50 square two, five zero zero negative, 10 square, one hundred and so on. So then we're going to go on down and say the total totalling up the square numbers in this case gives us the 38 600. If we take the population size, which is just one, two, three, four or five, six, seven, eight, nine, ten of them divided by ten, we're going to get the population variance, the three eight six zero. But again, these are like squared units. So if these were dollars, it'd be like square dollars. So if we take that and and take the square root of it, we get then the standard deviation. So we're taking the square root, which would be the three eight six zero, and we're square root, which would give us the 62 to 12 about or 62, 13. And so that's going to be in the billions.

But notice, I can't really compare that to what happened with this series of data. So that's often useful to us. But what we're going to be looking for oftentimes with our analysis is to divide that by the mean and give us the coefficient of variation. And so now this number is relevant to us, because when I compare the two items, that's giving us a relevant comparison. So we have different amounts, which you can imagine being different dollar amounts. But when I compare them out, this coefficient of variation gives us a number that gives a better kind of a variation of those different dollar amounts around. You know, basically the meaning can be a useful comparison to us.

This is telling us that these two data sets have a similarity, which we can't really get from, you know, the other the other calculations, the population variance or the standard deviation as easily. Now, Of course, you can calculate these with the calculations in Excel. We could take the mean of the first data set. Simply averaging up the data set equals average and then taking the data set, which would be the range of data one through 11. We can then take the standard deviation, which would be the steep drop if it's the population size of once again that data set giving us that three point one, one matching the three point one, one up top.

And then we could take the very variance which would be the V.A. P for the population of once again that data set giving us the nine point sixty five and the and then the coefficient of variation being calculated the same way as a top standard deviation divided by the mean. If we did that for a data set with the same kind of idea, we can do this with Excel, with the second data set over here and get a quick calculation. But remember and note that when you actually look at the data set, we can start to see pictorially actually, you know, the similarities with the data set. So it's actually useful to map them out sometimes this way because you can glean information and that's what you're trying to do a lot of times with a lot of different statistical situations. You're trying to. Picture the data, there's numbers that represent real things, right, and try to see it from different angles and mapping out the data if it's not too large and you have the capacity to do so and that way could actually be useful.

Standard Deviation, Variance, & Coefficient of Variation

Now we're going to look at those statistical concepts as a tool, typically for projections that we're going to be making out into the future. So there's multiple different scenarios we can think about this kind of analysis coming into place. We're going to start off with an advertising campaign here. And what we want to do is group what we think is going to happen into the future, into some components, because when we start to think about the future, what might happen from something like an advertising campaign and try to make projections about it, it can be very daunting to to try to predict what's going to happen to the future. One way we might do this is to say let's group the categories in likelihood of something like low average, high and very high for basic categories and then say what the standard in this case unit sales would be that basically within those categories.

So we're going to say, OK, if we if the advertising based on past experience and obviously a lot of this information is projections out into the future, therefore, we're going to look at the past experience as best we can and just do the best we can to kind of format and structure the data in such a way that we can we can wrap our mind around it and make as good a projection into the future as possible. So we're going to assume or look into and then get these 650 there. If the advertising campaign is not low, that's going to be our low results. Now, again, we might take past data and we might basically project that into the future, taking into consideration the current economy as well.

Then we'll take the average if it's an average campaign, 750 units high, 900 very high, we're going to be one thousand. So these are the markers at which we would determine if something, you know, is low average, high or very high. So then we want to assign probabilities or how likely we think that these outcomes will happen again. These probabilities are based on past experience and they're going to have to be estimates because we're making probabilities and guesses about what's going to happen into the future. But this is one way that we could structure this thought process in our mind so that we could get to and in essence, an expected value which will often need in order to do further assessments and further kind of calculations with regards to whatever we're talking about in this case, an advertising campaign, the unit sales then possibly being necessary for calculating how much inventory we need in that kind of stuff.

So we take the unit sales and we're going to multiply times to 20 percent. Now, these percentages, 20, 20, 30, 30 would be based on past experience and whatnot. They have to add up then, Of course, to 100 percent so that we could then apply our percentages. So then we'll simply take the 650 times the 20 percent. So let's just do one of them 650 times to point to 20 percent, the one 30 the 750 times 20 percent, 150, 900 times the 30 percent, seven to 70. And then the 1000 times that 30 percent is the 300. So now note that we hit these markers as to when something would be low, high average, very high applied the percentages. And this then is going to be what we will call our expected value. This is the one we're basically going to use.

And if we were then to kind of think forward and try to do projections on what our inventory needs to be and whatnot, as in this case, we're talking about an advertising campaign, the number of units that we might have to sell with. So then we come up to that. Now, you could think of that as the expected value, which is basically kind of the average or the mean when you think about our statistical type of terms. So then we're going to do our same calculation with our population variance. As we saw with the statistical analysis, there's going to be a faster way to do this. When you see this standard set up, note that oftentimes many problems might simply be asking you for this expected value.

You might use this oftentimes to come up or structure your mind around some set of information that you're projecting out into the future to get to the expected value, which you can then use for further analysis. For example, this might be further used once again for the calculation of inventory and how much manufacturing you might need or something like that. But we might have multiple sets of data. That we're combining together and we might want more statistical analysis other than this, which is basically the average, which would give us kind of the variance around the average. And so we'll take a look at those items and we'll do it with just one problem at a time right now. And then we'll do some comparisons which will make these calculations a little bit more clear.

So first, we're going to break this information out into kind of a list so it looks more like the list that we would basically be working with these statistical type of analysis and then we'll break it out in the format that will more commonly be used for these types of problems down below where we use these weightings. But first, let's break out this list, because I think this is one way to link math to the concepts that we're talking about here. Let's pretend we're going to break this out into a list of data and let's make out 10 items that have this structure of 20 percent, 20 percent, 30 percent, 30 percent. So if we have 10 items and we said 650 was 20 percent, then we're going to have two of them being the 650 the two items out of 10, 20 percent. And then we're going to say that the 750 once again, two of them at the 750, the 900 at 30 percent.

So we'll have three 900 in our series of ten data sets and then three one thousand at the thirty percent. So now we have a list of data that basically represents our formulas up top or our information up top with the populations represented in percentages. And then we can apply our formula, the same format we did here. So we had each unit minus the mean. So now we'll calculate the mean here and then we'll subtract that out so it'll look like this and the mean we already calculated with that 650 at the expected value. But if you see it in a list formula like this, how would you calculate the mean? Well, it would be 650 plus 650 plus 750 plus 750 plus 900 plus 900 plus 900 plus 1000 plus one thousand divided by the number of units or the population, which in this case was ten.

There's ten items here divided by ten and that would give us our 850. So that 850 then is the average or the mean, kind of like the center point that we're talking about, not the median, but the mean. And then we and then we're looking at the difference between the value and the means. So the 650 minus to 850 is the negative 200, 650, minus 850, same 750 minus to 850. Negative 100. Same here, 900 minus the 850 is 50. Same same same 1000. Minus the 850 is 150. So then we're going to square it. So now we're on this part of our formula, squaring each of the items. So if I was to square each item and let's just do one of them with the trusty calculator that will make the positive numbers, then I mean, the negative numbers positive and it will.

Amplify the results. And so we're going to say, let's say this is 200 negative and square it, there's forty thousand. So forty thousand there. Pulling this back over and if we squared all of them, we're going to do the same 40, they're one 1000, 10000, they're negative 100 square ten thousand fifty square, two thousand five hundred fifty square, two thousand five hundred 150 square 22 five and so on. So then we can sum this up. So if we sum these up, this one seventy five thousand, that's the numerator up top, then we're going to divide it by the number of units of the population, which was one, two, three, four, five, six, seven, eight, nine, ten. There's ten of them. So we'll take that and we'll divide it by the population size ten. That's going to give us our five. That is the variance that we talked about in the prior chapter.

Now it's in unit squares. So if we're talking about the units, we're talking units squared here. So oftentimes you would want to take the variance and take the square root. And that's what we call the standard deviation. So the standard deviation then is going to be in the units that we're talking about of the 132. So if I take then the square root, the one seven five oh and then square root, we get the one thirty two point two nine about. So there is that and that's going to be in the actual unit. So that gives us an idea about and that's in you know, in this case, units which were the units, the units of sales that we're going to have for our advertising campaign. And so that'll give us an idea of the disbursement around the mean and units that are typically relevant to us.

And then this last piece will not usually be relevant unless we have different things that we will be comparing, which we will do in the future, like two advertising campaigns that we were trying to compare. So that would then be the one thirty two point to nine divided by the 850, which would be about one five five six. You could represent this as a percent or decimal. That would be the coefficient of variation. So again, if I had two advertising campaigns and we had different different values for for the units, but we want to then see how similar they are with regards to their disbursement around the mean, which could give us a level of risk, which we'll talk about in the future, then that will be a relevant number.

And that's a really common kind of calculation in a lot of these types of calculations. This coefficient of variation will be practiced, just calculating it a couple of times and then we'll get into the comparisons in future practice problems. Now, you could do this in Excel if you did this in Excel and just put your little table down here and represent this in a table format, you can take the mean or average. That would be the average of our data set, which would be up top of these numbers, average of those numbers. That would be the mean or the average, which is also the expected value that we're talking about here. Eight fifty. The standard deviation would be equal to the Steve P and the Dot P could be A. S two, if it was a sample typically used in the population here.

If you want more information on statistical differences between population and sample a lot of information out there on those just purely mathematical concepts so you can search around on your favorite browser or YouTube and whatnot to check those out. But that would give us one thirty two point two nine matches here. And then we have the very variance which we can calculate at the AARP once again P population versus S, which would be a sample. We're using population here, which would be the seventeen five and then the coefficient of variation, same calculation, standard deviation divided by the mean or average or expected value. And that'll give us points one, five, five, six. So that's one way I think it's useful to kind of bridge into the way it will normally be presented here. Same calculation with our expected values up top.

And now let's basically think about it the way we would often format these types of problems. So if I took the 650, for example, times twenty percent, we'd get the one thirty. If we take the 750 times of twenty percent, we get one fifty. If we take the 900 times of thirty percent, we get the 270, the 1000 times the thirty percent. Three hundred. There's our 850 again. Which as we saw is basically the mean or the average. So we've got a bunch of different words for that one. It's a well-known concept and it's got many titles, many names, average expected value to live a long time and it's got a lot of history and a lot of different names. OK, so then we're going to go down here and figure it this way. Let's put our possibilities, the 650, the 750, the nine hundred and the one thousand just listing out our possibilities. We're in essence doing the same kind of concept or calculation.

Sorry to bounce around here of this population variance formula, but it's a little bit different format because we're going to apply the probabilities last basically, so you'll see the similarities. So the expected amount is now the 850, which is basically once again the average or the mean in essence. And then if we take the difference between these now, we got the 650 minus to 850, negative 200, 750 minus 850, negative 100 900, minus a 50 50 and the one thousand miles to 850 to 150, then we're going to square these items. So the 200 square. So let's do one of those in the calculator just for the fun of it, because it is good times. The 200 making it negative squared. Forty thousand. Wow. That was fun. That was fun. I wouldn't want to do another one, but no, I won't. So we got the one down.

The one hundred negative squared is the ten thousand to fifty squared is the two thousand five hundred the 150 squared 20 to five. Then we're going to apply the probabilities which are going to be the twenty twenty thirty thirty. So twenty, twenty, thirty, thirty. And that then gives us our end result of the forty thousand times to twenty percent, the eight thousand, the ten thousand times the twenty percent twenty two thousand five hundred times thirty percent 750 and the twenty to five times to thirty percent of the six seven five zero. And if we add those up population variance of the seventeen five which is the same result we got up top. So this is more the standard way that you will see these, although a little bit different of the calculation, as you can see, than just a series of numbers which were probably most used to.

When we're dealing with a which is a series of numbers possibly, or that's probably what you remember most when you're looking back on statistics. So as a series of numbers. So then we have the standard deviation, which is going to be the 132, in essence, taking the square root. So let's do that. And so say we're going to take the square root of one seven five oh oh and square root. So the root square is about one thirty two. It's been rounded. It's been rounded and then and so that's going to give us the same kind of concept we talked about before of the variance around, you know, the average of the mean. And then we got the expected value of the 150, basically the average or the mean, the 132 minus to 850 is rounded, 132 being rounded. It's going to give us that coefficient of variation. Not really helpful for us when we only have one project here, but when we have multiple projects, it can give us an idea about the the spread around the mean of multiple projects once again, when having different basically outcomes or dollar amounts, but similar or we want to see how similar the spread is around the average or the mean or the expected value.

Expected Value, Standard Deviation, & Coefficient of Variation

We have our information up top going through the calculations down below. In a prior chapter, we took a look at the statistical tools for basically analyzing a set of data that we'll be using as we do our projections into the future. This is the second of a similar problem, so we'll do it a bit faster. Here we have our advertising campaign. Note that this is one of many different types of scenarios you might be using in order to group your information or group your ideas about what might happen in the future into a thought process so you can get some results and move forward. When you're looking at an advertising campaign, then you might be thinking about the advertising campaign.

Of course, having an impact on the unit sales that you're going to have is what you need to calculate so that you can then determine how much inventory you need and possibly how much production you need to make if you're doing a production type of situation. So one way to do that is to try to take your future information, group it into the likely results and get some categories as to what would it look like if you had a low outcome, an average outcome, an outcome or a very high outcome? Now, note, you might use more categories or you might use less categories than this, right? You're trying to group this into an information, a set of numbers that you could basically get an average from.

And then we need to predict what our unit sales would be, which would be based on possibly prior information, prior advertising campaigns to see what the low outcome would generally be, the average, the high and the very high, so that we can get the 700 to 800, the 1000 to 1600, then assign our probabilities, which once again might be based on prior data and then taking into consideration the current market and what we think is going to happen in the future. And in this case, we're going to say thirty, thirty, thirty ten and then we can calculate our expected value. And that's basically the value that we can then use possibly to figure the next step out of whatever we need this number for.

If it's for budgeting, for example, we might need it then so that we can then calculate the unit sales and our inventory and how much we're going to buy for inventory or possibly production and whatnot. So we're going to take the 700 and then multiply it by thirty percent. That's going to give us the 210, the 800 on the average times, the 30 percent, the 240, the high of the 1000 at the 30 percent, the 300 and the 1600 at the 10 percent is one hundred and sixty. So one sixty notice Of course, that the sum of the percentages have to add up to 100 percent because we are in essence taking an average, which we're going to call the expected value. So you can think about it as statistical terms average mean in essence or in this case, the expected value.

So that might be kind of where you stop in some kind of scenario. You're trying to get that number once again to figure out your further budget or something like that into the future. Or you might be comparing different advertising campaigns and want to think about the variance from basically the mean.

So then we might want the population variance, the standard deviation and the coefficient of variation. So first, let's think about that by breaking this out into our numbers series again, like we did in the prior chapter. And then we'll go down here and do it in this format that will generally be presented with these types of problems that we have, these weights that will be lined out.

The idea of this first step is to line it up in a statistical kind of format that we would be used to when we just have a number set and then apply these calculations to do these calculations on including the standard deviation and so on. So we're going to pick up our numbers series. So we're going to say that this 700, if we had ten numbers, let's just make a series of ten numbers and weight them at thirty, thirty, thirty ten, ten numbers would be 700, 700, 700. Then the 800 we have thirty percent. So that would be 800, 800, 800 or three of them. One thousand thirty percent. We're going to have three of those and then the 10 percent at the one thousand six that would be the one out of the ten.

One thousand six. Then we can calculate the mean or the average and we'll be doing our comparison between the values and the mean. In essence, this calculation up top, taking each of the values minus the mean or the. Now, we already calculated it here, that's basically the expected value, but let's calculate it the normal average way here, if we had 10 numbers, it would be the 700 plus the 700 plus the 700 to 800 plus to 800 plus to 800 plus the one thousand plus the 1000 plus the one thousand plus the one six divided by the number of numbers. The population is divided by ten in this case, because there's 10 numbers there. There are nine, ten once again, that being the expected value that means the mean or the average, you could see it as so there it is all the way down.

Then we'll take the difference. So we'll take the seven hundred minus the nine. Ten negative to ten. Same here. Same here. The 800 minus the nine. Ten is the negative one tenth. Same here. Same here. One thousand minus the 1990. Same here. Same here. And then the one thousand six hundred minutes to nine. Ten or the six ninety. So now we're going to square it. We're basically at this point now we're going to square these items. So let's go ahead and square each one of them. I'll do one of them just for the fun of it with the trusty calculator trusty calculator square. In this thing, we're taking the 210 negative squared and that's the four to four to four one.

So there we have that. If we take the two squares, the forty one note, the squaring, Of course, removes the negative number and amplifies the result here. Forty for one and then the one ten negative squared is the twelve one, the one ten twelve one and then so on the ninety squared eight thousand one hundred ninety. Same thing. Same thing. And then the ninth, the 690 ninety squared notice when you get the larger number Of course the squaring has a significant impact. The 476 one hundred. So then if we add these up or at the six six nine eight zero zero zero six six nine thousand, we're going to divide that by the population, which Of course is in our formula up top, the population being the ten numbers, ten numbers here. So ten on the population.

The six, six, nine thousand divided by ten is the sixty six nine, that being the population variance. So that gives us an idea of the variance, but it's in squared units. So what we would like to do oftentimes is take the standard deviation, which would be the square root of that. So we'll take the square root of that. So if I did that, we take these six six nine zero square roots and it gives us about the two fifty eight point sixty five to fifty eight point sixty five on the square of the root. And then that'll give us an idea of, you know, the spread from the mean and units that are applicable here instead of the squared units. And then we if we had multiple ad campaigns, which we'll see in the future, we might want the coefficient of variation which would be calculated by taking that number divided by the mean, the nine 10, the mean we calculated up top, which was could be called the average, could be called the mean, could be called the expected value.

And this number, the coefficient of variation will be more useful to us when we do a comparison. We'll see that in the future. But that's a common calculation in these types of practice problems. So we want to get used to getting to it at this point. Now, you could do this in Excel as well. So you might see in Excel, someone just listed out a set of numbers such as this. If you had our data set up top, the mean or the average, which is the average of these numbers here, which would be this formula average of the group of numbers, that would be our data set that would give us once again, the nine 10. The standard deviation would be the Steve P note that there's a standard deviation for the population and one for a sample which are slightly different.

I won't get into the differences. Now, if you want to take a look at it, take a, you know, search around on your favorite browser. There is a lot of information on that on YouTube and whatnot. And then we've got the variance. So the variance is in the varicorp once again, P versus S for us because we're taking the population rather than the sample and we're taking the same data range. So there's our sixty six nine and then the coefficient of variation calculated the same way, which would simply be the standard deviation divided by the mean average or expected value. So now it is calculated the way it would normally be done here and you'll see the similarities with the calculation we did up top.

So if we take the seven hundred times thirty percent, we get the 210 again, the 800 times 30 of the two for the one thousand times a thousand three hundred and the one thousand six hundred times ten is the one sixty for the expected value of the nine ten. Let's take that same information down here and put that seven. The 800. One thousand. One thousand six hundred. And then take a look at our expected value. This is our average, in essence, you'll recall from the prior chapter, which we calculated up here at the expected value of the nine ten. And if we compare all these to the expected value, taking the difference, you see a similarity with the step we did up top with this whole series of numbers, but this time down below, we're going to apply the probabilities at the end. So now we're going to say the difference. The 700 minus the nine ten is negative to ten, 800 minus to 910.

Negative one ten. The one thousand minus the nine ten is ninety and the one thousand six hundred minus the nine. Ten is six ninety then we'll square them. Let's just do one of them for the fun of it again. We did this last time. We'll square it again. Let's do the square. This is going to be the two one zero negative and then making this a little larger. So I see the squaring thing squared 44 one. There we have that squaring, the one, Tim, would be the 12 one square in the 90 would be the eight thousand one and square and the six ninety would be the 476 one. Then we'll apply our probabilities, which once again are the thirty, thirty, thirty ten. So thirty, thirty, thirty ten. So we did this basically on the last step.

Now the probabilities and we multiply those times, the squared items. So the forty four one times the thirty percent is thirteen to thirty the twelve one times thirty percent the three six three zero, the eight one time thirty percent to four three zero and the 476 one times the ten percent forty seven, six, ten. Then we're going to, we're going to add those up. That'll give us our population variance of the sixty six nine which matches what we got up to the 66 nine population variance, then we'll take the standard deviation square root of it. So the same point where we're at at this time. So do that here, make a larger calculator so I could see the square root thingy making me think that's the sixty six nine and then the square root thingy is the two fifty eight point sixty five.

And then we'll take the total expected value which is like the mean or the average to get the coefficient of variation, which once again will be more useful when we have multiple projects which we'll take a look at in future chapters. But you want to get used to that calculation, how to get there, because it's often going to be applicable with these types of problems.

Oftentimes, they might simply give you the standard deviation, the expected value, make you calculate something like the coefficient of variation, and then do an analysis comparing multiple different things with that coefficient. And we'll get to some of those types of problems in the future. But for now, you want to see where this fits into the rest of this typical kind of statistical calculation and how you might do it in multiple ways, how you might tie it into a normal type of series of numbers. So it all links together. It all clicks and makes some sense. And that way it'll stick in your memory, hopefully a bit longer.

Expected Value, Standard Deviation, & Coefficient of Variation

Closing the icon information is going to be up top, are going to go through the calculations then on down below. This is our third practice problem with a similar scenario. So we'll go, we'll go a bit faster at it. We want to get an idea, a feel for the layout so we could set these things up fairly quickly.

We're going to be projecting into the future. This is going to be a way for us to try to use some statistical kind of analysis in order to make the projections into the future. We can apply these to different things, different characteristics, which we will do in future chapters, and we want to get the format down to do so. So we have our possibilities down below. We're imagining the advertising campaign. We got the categories of bad, good and very good.

Note that the categories are not as important as, Of course, the numbers within the categories, but they can give you an idea of what we're talking about in terms of the category names. We then want to measure what it means to be in these categories with whatever we're going to measure by, in this case being the unit sales. So with advertising campaigns, this would often be useful or necessary so that we can continue on with our budgeting plan because we need to know how many we're going to sell in order to know how many we need to buy to have our inventory. And if we make the inventory, then we would need to know how much we need to make for a certain time period. This would be the starting point for our budgeting type of information. So important numbers then.

So you also could have more than three categories here. We could have anywhere from like one to five is kind of typical and then come up with our statistical kind of thought process. And we then would need to assign the probabilities to those categories. The probabilities then must add up to 100. So in this case, we're going to say bad is the 600 good? It's going to be a very good 800. 1400. Where would we get that information possibly from prior advertising campaigns and or then projecting out into the future, starting off with past data if we have it, and then project out into the future? Just giving our best guess and categorizing where we would be under different scenarios, then we want to wait for the likelihood for those scenarios to be bad, we're going to say the 30 percent good or average, probably that would be the 50 percent. You would kind of expect that one to be the larger of the percentages. Right.

And then very good at the twenty percent, the percentages needing to add up to 100 percent expected value, then being the 600 times the 30 percent or the one hundred and eighty the for the 800 times the fifty percent or the four hundred eighty one thousand four hundred twenty to twenty percent or the 280 adding up the 180, the 400 and the 210, we get up to the 860 note that 860 is basically kind of like the average or the mean as well. Basically go to and try to get a better handle of by taking this data and putting it into a normal kind of data, set down below a list of numbers that we can do our statistical kind of calculations on. And it'll be more similar to the calculations you might see in a statistics Book where you might start off with a list of numbers that you want to apply some statistical analysis to.

So let's reset these numbers into basically a list of ten numbers just to get a feel for that. And then we'll go down after that and do that. It is kind of a more normal type of calculation that we might see in this and this set in corporate finance. So let's take these numbers. If we say, OK, if there's a thirty weighting, a 50 percent weighting and a 20 percent rating and I had ten numbers, then it would look something like this. The six hundred we're going to imagine is three out of the ten, right. Three out of the ten is going to be the 600. Then we're going to imagine the four out of the ten or the five out of the ten here because that's fifty percent.

So five out of ten. And then the last would be the one thousand four hundred. What happened two times out of ten adding up. These are ten items that we're talking about here. Then we can calculate the mean of this. Now what we're going to be looking into is basically this formula, which is the population variance. So we're going to be taking each of the items compared to the mean or the average square divided by the population, which are ten numbers that we just put together at this point. So the. Or the average, if we were to take these 10 numbers and do our calculation on that, let's do that 600 plus 600 plus 600 plus 800 plus 800 plus 800 plus 800 plus one four zero zero plus one four zero zero equals the eight six zero zero. We're going to divide by the population, which is ten of them.

There's ten of these numbers here divided by ten that's going to give us our average or mean of 860. Remember, that's kind of like the center point, not the median, not like the middle number, but the average. Right. That's going to be the average that we're looking for. So we're going to take that all the way down as the 860 for the mean or the average. Then we're going to take the difference. Subtracting this out. We're basically up here now. The difference for each of the numbers to the mean, if we take the six hundred minus the 860, we get a negative 260, bringing this all the way down to the eight hundred minus the 860, we get 60. And then we take this all the way down to the last couple where we have the one thousand four hundred minus the 860 is the 560. Then we apply our squaring.

So that's going to be here in our calculation. We're going to do our squaring squaring thing now. That's what we're in the square thing. And so we're going to then take the calculator up. We'll take the two six zero squares and that's going to be the sixty seven six sixty seven six. So we're going to say there it is, 67 six squaring these. That, Of course, removes the negative here. So I didn't put a negative in the calculator, but the negative goes away when you're squared. That's part of the reasoning, the rationale rationale. So the 60s negative, 60 squared is the three thousand six negative 60 squared and so on. And in the 540 square, 291 six hundred.

Then if we add these up, then we add all these up. There's eighty four thousand now. That's our numerator basically up top and we're going to divide it by the population which we saw was ten because there's 10 items, there's ten numbers of things. That's the population size. So if we take the eight zero four thousand divided by ten, we're at the variance of the eighty thousand four hundred. Remember that? That's kind of like a squared unit. So typically we'll take the standard deviation, which is the square root of that, those square roots meaning we're going to pull in that number, the eight zero four zero zero. And then the square root is going to be 283 55. So there we have that.

And then we might want the mean here, the 860, to get to the bottom line of the coefficient of variation, which you might see presented as a percent or a decimal point three two nine seven, this number becoming important to us when we do comparisons of multiple projects, such as multiple advertising projects, which we don't have yet, but we'll do shortly. Note that you can also see these calculations just in Excel so you can have functions for these calculations that you might just see it like this would be the mean or the average Damu would be the average. The average formula equals the average of the series of numbers, which would be just these 10 numbers. The series of numbers would give you that 860.

Once again, you can have the standard deviation, which would be the Steve Dopy. The Dot P stands for population versus sample. We're using population here. If you want to know the difference between the population and the sample. There's many, many statistical kinds of things on YouTube and the Internet. You can look at that great material, Fort Worth Worth up to. Then we got the variance and that's going to be you can calculate that with a formula which would be equal to Vahdat P once again, the P stands for the population versus the sample. So we're talking about a whole population versus a sample population and that would be the same series of numbers and that would give you the eighty thousand four hundred matching the eighty thousand four hundred up top.

Then we can calculate the coefficient of variation the same way we did up top, just taking the standard deviation divided by the mean standard deviation over divided by the mean. So then let's do the same kind of thing with the standard corporate. Finance kind of layout where we're going to do the probabilities at the end, well, we'll just twist around the calculations a little bit. So this time, same kind of thing, getting to the same result, but different methods, shorter method, this time the standard type of method. So we're now going to have the 600, the 800, the 1400, same same unit sales we're expecting for our three categorisations here. The expected value then, which we now see, is kind of like the average, the mean, the expected value.

It's a well-known figure. It goes by many names, 860. And then the difference is going to be the 600 minus the 860 is the negative to 60, 80 minus the 860, negative 60. And then the one thousand four minus the 860 is the five hundred and forty. Then we will square it. So we're going to take the 260 squared or the negative to 60 squared. Gives us the sixty seven six, the sixty squared gives us the 3600 and the 540 squared gives us that two nine one six hundred. Then we're going to apply our probabilities at the end here, then we're going to apply the probabilities at the end, which is going to be the 30, 50, 20, 30, 50, 20, 67, six times 30 percent. Twenty thousand to eighty. Three thousand six hundred times fifty percent. One thousand eight hundred.

The two ninety one. 600 times twenty percent. Is that 58 320. So then we have our variance which will be calculated as the twenty thousand to 80 plus these three numbers. I won't say the numbers, those three numbers add up to eighty thousand four hundred. Same variance we got to up top. So now we're basically back to the same point we did up top with this different kind of format of the calculation, standard deviation, then square root of the eighty thousand four hundred, the two eighty three fifty five. Same calculation we had up top. Then we're going to take that, divide it by the mean or the average, which we're now calling the expected value we got here and we got up top here. And that's going to give us the coefficient of variation.

Now, remember, depending on the problem you are using, you might end up having a problem that just stops here. You need the expected value. That's what you need for something like inventory. So you can do your budgeting going forward. Possibly. But if you're kind of comparing, then, you know, one option to another, which we'll talk about in future chapters, then this is typically the number that will be helpful for that, because that's going to help you to to compare different numbers that possibly have different kind of dollar amount or unit unit amounts with them. And you can kind of measure the spread away from the mean with the coefficient of variation.

Coefficient of Variation Three Investment Alternatives

We're going to imagine a situation. We're going to have three different types of investment opportunities and we're going to go through a similar type of analysis we've seen in prior chapters to try to get an idea of what the outcomes might be for each of those three. So the three outcomes then or the process that we will be using for the investments is to try to think about the range of what a good return would be, the not so good and a very good type of returns.

You don't really need that. The main categories over here, you need basically the return categories. And then we'll basically put together what we expect to be the case under a not so good, good and very good type of scenario that will typically want between one and five types of categories and then wait for those categories in some way.

You might ask, well, how would you do that? You might look at past performance to see what happens in the past and then make projections or predictions about what's going to happen in the future and then see if you can get basically probabilities or likelihood the structure can start to formulate or frame your thinking so that you can hopefully make a logical decision about them. So we're going to do that for basically an option one, option two, option three. I imagine these three different investments with three different alternatives that we are imagining could happen and the probabilities of those happening. So all this is projections. So when I'm talking about the probabilities and whatnot, Of course, in these amounts and the returns, we don't know.

We're looking out into the future. We're trying to format our thoughts in as systematic a way as possible to get to as clear a thought process, to try to think about the future as we can. So we're going to say that it's not good. We got the 400 times to 20 percent that's going to give us the 80. The 800 times the 20 percent is the one. And the very good is going to be our most likely option. We believe possibly the economy is going up or something like that. And we're thinking that it's going to be what we expect to happen. One thousand three fifty times the 60 percent is 810. Obviously, all the percentages need to be added up to one hundred percent. That's going to be our expected return. So we expect then the return, based on this analysis, to be the one thousand fifty for option two.

We're going to say seven hundred. If it's not a good average, we're going to say it is the 1400 tonnes to 20 percent or the 280 and then the very effective two thousand fifty times to 60 percent is the one thousand to thirty. Obviously, these add up to 100 percent as well. Note that we have different dollar amounts between option one and option two. Investment one, investment two. However, the probabilities are the same. And then in investment three, we're thinking we have 750 at forty percent. So now we have different probabilities here. So the 40 percent times the 7300, the two to the two five five zero times the 40 percent is the 1020 and the four thousand fifty times the twenty percent is the 810 for a total of twenty one thirty, these adding up to one hundred as well.

So between these three, the last option has our greatest expected return. We've got the two thousand 130 versus the 1000, 650 and one thousand fifty. The next thing we might want to look at then is going to be the level of risk. So we might want to consider and think about what's going to be the level of risk, what's going to be the level of variation then from this number, which is basically the expected value, which you could think about as kind of the mean or the average average mean the same thing and the basically expected value in this term and is in essence the same thing as well. Now, note, if this one had the highest expected value, it could possibly come out to the situation where there's actually less risk for the higher one.

So if this one had less risk and a higher expected value, then it would be a fairly clear choice. But if you're in a situation where this one has higher expected value but more risk, which is often the case, that's when you're trying to compare between what you want to do. Right. If this one had a higher expected value and less risk, then not really a question if it has a higher expected value and more risk. Then the question is, do we want to be taken on the higher the more risk because of the higher potential value that we could have and that could depend on what your risk aversion is. Are you risk averse or do you not mind risk and what your portfolio basically looks like, what you're looking for in terms of return versus risk.

So let's break that down a little bit further, then we're going to take this down a bit differently here. We're going to say the returns on this first investment. We're back to the first and best investment now of the 400, the 800, the 1000, 350. We're looking at the expected value, which is basically the average.

And comparing that out now, that's the expected value of the 1050. And we'll take that all the way down to the four hundred minus the one thousand fifty is the negative 650. The 800 minus the one thousand fifty is the negative 250 and the 1000, 350 minus to 1050 is the 300. Now, we're going to go through our process and square that. So let's do the first one just with our trusty calculator here, squaring the first one.

So we're going to make it squared, which will be six fifty negative and then square it, which is going to be for two to five hundred. So we're going to say that's going to be for two to five. The two fifty squared is negative to fifty squared. It's a positive 62 five, 300 squared is the ninety thousand. Then we're going to apply out our probabilities, which are the 2068 in this case. Twenty, twenty, sixteen. So the four to five hundred times twenty percent is the eighty four or five hundred. The 6500 times the twenty percent is the twelve thousand five hundred and ninety thousand times the sixty percent is the fifty four thousand dollars. Then if we add those up the eighty four or five, the twenty five, the 54000 we get the one fifty one thousand that's going to be the variance, it's in squared units.

So then oftentimes we want to take these standard deviations, which is the square root of that number. So if we took the one fifth one oh and square routinized it, which would be this little key, that would be the three eighty eight point five nine. And then we're going to take that and compare it to the expected value, which is basically the mean or median to give us the coefficient of variation. So in essence, we're taking that number divided by the one zero five zero, which we calculated up top. That gives us the point, three oh one about round it.

So if this number then is not very helpful in and of itself, but when compared to the other investment options, could give us an idea and we'll apply that idea to basically the level of risk involved. So let's take a look at the second one and do the same thing then.

Same thing for the second one. Returns are going to be now the 700, the 1000 for the two zero five zero. We take the expected value, which is the 1006 fifty all the way down. Take the difference between the two. The seven hundred minus the one thousand six fifty is the negative 950. The one thousand four hundred minus the one thousand six fifty is the negative 250 and the 2050 minus to 1000, 650 is 400. We're then going to square it, square all of them, those three numbers. So let's take the nine five zero. We're going to make that negative and then square it. We got the nine to five and nine to five and then we've got the 250 squared 62 five. The 400 square is the 160 probabilities then applied.

That's going to be the twenty twenty, sixteen, twenty, twenty sixteen. We got the nine to five times the twenty percent is the one hundred and eighty five or six. 62, five times twenty percent. Twelve thousand five. And one hundred and sixty thousand times that sixty percent is 96000. We add those three numbers up and we get to the two eighty nine thousand. That being the variance then we're going to take the standard deviation which would be the square root of that to eighty nine thousand, take the square of the root root in the square root and that's going to be the five thirty nine fifty nine about. And then we compare that to the expected value we got to up top to get to our coefficient of variation.

That's where our key focus is going to be divided out by the one six five zero, the point three to eight five eight, so that we're going to do a comparison between that in the first one in a second. But let's do the last one first so we will do the comparisons. But hold on. Let's do the last one first. I know it's exciting to now compare those two, but we'll do this and then we'll compare patients, patients. We have these 750 and then the two five five zero, the five four zero five oh expected value. That's going to be the two one three zero. Then the difference, 750 minus to two one three zero and negative one three eight zero two five five zero minus two two one three zero is the Ford twenty in the four zero five zero minus the two one three zero is the one nine two zero square. In those items, then let's just do the first one again, we're going to take the one three eight oh negative and square, it is the one million nine or four for the four, 20 squared is the one 176 for and the one nine two zero squared is the three million six eight six four applying the probabilities that be in the forty forty 20.

So the one million nine four four times the 40 percent is the 961 760, the 176 four times the 40 percent, 70000, 560 and the three million six eight six, four times the 20 percent is the 737 to eight zero. Adding those three numbers up, we're at one million five six to nine six. That being the variance, we're then taking the standard deviation, the square root of the variance. So we'll take them to one five six nine six o square root. And that's going to be the one to five, two or one, two, five, three about rounded, and then we'll compare that to the expected value, which we got up top, the mean or the average, in other words.

So taking that divided by the two one three zero gives us the point five eight eight one, which is the coefficient of variation. So now let's consider those three. This one's going to be the least risky because it has the lowest coefficient of variation. So this one's the least risky. And then the second least risky is the 37 01. And the third least risky is going to be this item down here according to the coefficient of variation. So remember, with regards to the return, this one down here had the highest expected return, but it also has the most risk related to it. So if we take a look at these two up top, we've got the 1050 and the 1000, 650.

And now between these two, you notice this one has a higher expected return than this one and it's less risky. So in that case, it's not it's not usually a difficult decision. In that case, if our expected return is higher and it's less risky than most likely, we would want to be choosing the second option as opposed to the first option that can happen. And again, oftentimes when you think about finance, you start thinking, well, you know, the higher the risk, the higher the reward. And that's true. But just remember that, you know, the risk going up does not necessarily mean that the reward is necessarily higher. That's just it, just so you know, you've got to weed out the bad ones, which means that that's not the case.

When that is not the case, when the risk goes up and the reward is not higher, the potential reward is not higher. That's not good. The question is, which ones do have a higher basically return with that, with the increased risk? Right. So between these two, you'd probably be looking at the second one and then you'd be comparing the second one and the third one. And then this one is a situation where you have a higher expected return and it's more risky, which would be then the question would be, do we want to take on the added risk in order for the potential expected future return? And when you're asking that question now that you've narrowed down to that being the question, then the question is, what are you going to be a risk averse type of personality? Or are you not concerned about risk in order to get a higher return or possibly have the probability of getting a higher return? And or what am I looking for with regards to the other factors that are in my current situation, whether that be a portfolio or my business structure? Does this fit well within my overall business structure, what I need with regard to risk level and where my current investments are possibly with regards to risk level and my diversification on a broader kind of spectrum.

Coefficient of Variation & Investment Risk

Now, when we think about different types of investments in different types of opportunities that we might be comparing, the coefficient of variation is typically what we're going to be using to think about the level of risk. So we talked about how to get to some of these components, which are the expected return and the standard deviation in prior chapters. We're going to say that they are given at this point so that we can compare multiple different scenarios. If you have questions then about how to get to the expected return, what is the expected return and so on, and the standard deviation and so on. Take a look at the prior chapters. We're going to have those given.

So that will calculate the coefficient of variation. You'd have to think about the level of risk between different types of investment options. So the coefficient variation would then be calculated. Once we have these two numbers quite easily calculated, we'll just divide them out. We're going to take the standard deviation, the one three zero zero divided by the one seven zero zero that would give us if we round here, point seven six five, you might see it represented as a percent or a decimal. And then we're going to take these seven thousand divided by the three one zero zero zero. That's going to give us the point two to six about then we have the nine thousand nine thousand divided by the thirty one thousand. And that's going to give us the point, two nine zero.

Then we're going to be picking up the 50000. The sorry. Twenty three thousand divided by the 50000 that's going to give us three point four six two zero. And then finally, finally, eighty eight thousand divided by the one 76000 gives us the point five. Now, then the next step, which is probably the one to be focused on more with a problem like this, is to rank these from a level of risk. So if we were to rank this one here, I'm going to remove this. This one would be the lowest number. So the lower the number, typically, the less the amount of the risk because we have the less kind of variation from the center point of the average or the expected return.

So this would be one. The second the three this number three over here would be two with regard to risk. This one would be three with regard to risk, four with regard to risk and five, with regard to risk just going from lowest to highest. Now, then, if you think about that further, just notice that the expected returns are quite different. This is kind of what we would expect the return to be based on our calculations. If you want to go more into that, you can look at prior chapters. But that's what we kind of expect the return to be kind of like the average return or the mean. Obviously, the fifth one here is much higher. So if we were going by expected return, then we would think, number five, we would pick the number five, number four, and then these two are the same and then number one last.

So if I didn't have anything on the coefficient of variation, I wasn't looking at risk at all and I was simply looking at return. Then Of course, this one would be the best, this one. And then these two are the same. And then this one up top, the one seventy six thousand. In other words, than the fifty thousand. Then there's two for thirty one thousand and one for seventeen thousand would then be last. If I look at just the ranking with regards to return then this one at the point two to six which is actually the thirty one thousand would be the lowest with return and the best in that case for four less levels of risk. And then the two, then the two points, the two nine zero would be number two. Number three, the fifty thousand for point four six zero. And then number four, the one seventy six thousand.

Now if you consider both of those, obviously, if the risk is going up, we would only consider picking that one if the expected return was also going up. So if I look at this one, for example, that has the least amount of risk, it's at thirty one thousand. The second one here that has the second about to risk a higher amount of risk has the same expected return. So between those two, you would think that we would pick the first one because it has the same expected return and a lower amount of risk. So why take on, in other words, a higher amount of risk when the expected return is the same? Would be kind of the general idea would be the general notion.

So between those two, you would think you pick the first one. And then if you go from here to number three, we get now we got a fifty thousand return and the increased risk. So now the question, Of course, would be while the expected return goes from thirty one thousand to fifty thousand, then is it worthwhile for us to have that higher expected return, given the fact that the risk is also going up? Right. And then if I go from three to four, this one has a substantial difference in the expected return, but also a difference in the risk assessment. So once again, the question is, well, now the expected returns are quite a bit higher here.

Is that worthwhile to take on the added level of risk? And then number five up top is actually the most risky. So this one, why would you pick at this one at all is the question. You probably wouldn't pick number five because it has the lowest expected amount of return and also is the most risky. And remember, that could happen. So it doesn't whenever you think about stocks, you're always thinking you're always hearing people or any type of investment. You gotta spend money to make money. You've got to take on a risk. You know, the reward comes with risk and there's truth to that. But don't don't let that lead you to believe that simply a higher increase in risk means that there's a higher expected return, the higher increase in risk, you know, you can have risk going up to the moon and not have a higher expected return.

Right. You know, so you want to make sure that if you are taking on higher risk, you're doing so with the idea that the expected return is going up to. That's why you're willing to take on the higher risk. If the higher risk is going up and the expected return is not going up, then that's what you want to weed out. You don't want to, that's not where you want to be, then that's going to be the objective. So it is true that typically the chances for higher expected returns typically will have higher risk related to them. So you want in the question once you weed those out, is to pick those out. But it is possible to see higher risk go up quite possible clearly to have risk go up without having the expected returns go up. And those are the ones that you kind of want to weed out. And then come to the decision as to whether the expected return being higher is worth the added level of risk when you're comparing multiple different investment opportunities.

Coefficient of variation Two Project Alternatives

We'll go through the calculations then down below, we are imagining we have two projects that we are considering and we want to do our analysis side by side for the projects. We're going to do our ratio type of thought process for that analysis to get the expected value and then to be looking at the coefficient, possibly to think about the amount of risk that could be involved. So we have the project one cash flow. These are what we are projecting the cash flows to be in the future. And we got our probabilities related to them. So the same kind of scenario we're projecting out into the future. We're trying to think what is going to happen into the future and then trying to think about the likelihood of that happening.

So obviously, we don't know. We would have to look at the past and see what has happened in the past and consider the economic conditions into the future and think if we can put down in some systematic way what we think the probabilities of particular outcomes would be. This is one way to structure our thought process as we make our decisions into the future. We have that for Project one and then Project two, and then we'll do some comparing and contrasting between the two. So let's take a look at Project one. First, we have the cash flows. We're going to assume the cash flows at the nine hundred the one thousand eight to one thousand nine, the two thousand six.

And then we have our probabilities for them. Again, we don't know what these probabilities are. We're estimating into the future. This is one way to structure our estimates as we think about this into the future. And also note that we could have four numbers here. We could have three numbers here. We could have, you know, usually less than 10% on the basically expected cash flows. And then, Of course, applying our probabilities to them, probabilities, having to add up them to 100 percent. So we've got the forty, 20, 20, 20 in this case, and then we have our expected value. So 900 times 20 percent is 180. The one thousand eight hundred times the 40 percent is the 720.

The one thousand nine hundred times of twenty percent is the 380 and the 2600 times the 20 percent is the 520, the 180, the 720, the 380, the 520. Those add up to one thousand eight hundred than our expected value. So based on this information, this is what we would expect to happen. This is kind of our average value, in other words, or the mean. And then we want to think about what the variation would be from from that average point so that when we compare it to the second project, we can look at two things, the expected value here, as well as basically the variation from that midpoint, from that average, from that mean, from that expected value, which could give us an idea of of the level of risk involved.

So let's do that same kind of thing so we can get to that variation down here. So the work got the cash flows once again, the 900 to 1800 to 1900, the twenty six, the expected value, which you can imagine being basically kind of like the average. That's one thousand eight hundred all the way down. We're going to compare each of our items to that one thousand eight hundred the nine hundred minus the one thousand eight hundred negative, nine hundred eighty one thousand eight hundred minus one thousand eight hundred is zero one thousand nine hundred minus one thousand eight hundred one hundred two thousand six hundred minus one thousand eight hundred is eight hundred.

Then we will square it. So the 900 negative 900 squared, let's just do one of these to pick one of them up and the trusty calculator making sure we have a squared button. Nine hundred negative 900 squared is the one ten or the eight ten thousand zero square to zero. One hundred squared is ten thousand eight hundred squared is 640. Then we're going to pick up our probabilities, which are the 2014 2020. So that's 2014 2020. Let's just pull that up here. There we have those then multiply in the eight, ten times the twenty percent. We have 162, the zero times the forty percent is zero. One hundred or ten thousand times twenty percent. Two thousand six forty times to twenty percent.

One twenty eight thousand. Adding those up gives us the variance of the two ninety two thousand that. Number is squared units, however, we typically want the standard deviation then, so we would do that by taking the square root. The two nine two zero zero zero square rooted gives us about the five forty thirty seven. And then we're going to compare that to the expected value, which is kind of like the mean or the average. So we take that number, divide it by the one eight oh and that then gives us the point three zero zero to about. So we got the point three zero zero. You could see this in a percent, could see it in a decimal. That number is what we can use to compare it to the second project to consider that risk kind of level.

Same thing for a project, too. Now let's take the project into two numbers. Here's the flow. Here's the probabilities that we came up with to be projecting out into the future. Let's calculate the expected value then cash flows that we came up with, the five hundred the 900 that one thousand 8th of 2004, the two thousand nine. Note that we have five numbers here as opposed to up top when we had the four categories up top. We do not need an even level of categories because what we're doing is getting to that expected value. So whatever level or however many categories we think would be most appropriate to get the most accurate expected value that we can think of, that's what we will do.

Then we got our probabilities, which we said were ten, thirty, ten, thirty and twenty. These have to add up, Of course, to 100 percent to make any sense when we want to make sense, since it needs to be made sense. So we have five hundred times the 10 percent is 15. We have 900 times that. 30 percent is 270. We have 1800 times the 10 percent is one eighty. The two thousand four hundred times thirty seven. The thirty percent is 720. The two thousand nine hundred times the twenty percent is the five eighty. Adding up the outer column we get to that one thousand eight hundred. That's our expected value.

Now Of course we can compare the expected values of the two to projects, the two investments, the one with the higher expected value being typically the better one. However, we also want to take into consideration the level of risk that could be involved. One way to get an idea of that is to do our calculation. Similar calculation we have down here for the second option, cash flows, same cash flows as we had up top expected value. The average or the mean basically is that one thousand eight hundred. We take the difference between each expected value. The 500 minus the one thousand eight hundred is negative one thousand three hundred nine hundred minus the one thousand eight hundred negative, nine hundred one thousand eight hundred minus 1800 is zero 2400. Minus one thousand eight hundred is six hundred two thousand nine hundred.

Minus one thousand eight hundred is one thousand one hundred. Then we will square each item. Let's just do the first one to practice the squaring, making sure we have a squared button on the calculator so we pick up the one three zero zero, make it negative one three zero zero and square it one million six ninety. There we have that. We do that all the way down, 900 squared one 810000 zero square to zero six hundred squared is three hundred and sixty thousand one thousand one hundred squared is one million two hundred and ten thousand. Then we apply our probabilities of ten thirty ten, thirty, twenty, ten, thirty, whatever that was. There it is.

Then we multiply that out. So the one million 690 times that ten percent is going to give us the one ninety six thousand, the eight, ten times the thirty percent to forty three thousand point zero times ten percent is zero and then the three hundred sixty thousand times of thirty percent is the one zero eight thousand and then the one million to ten times the twenty percent is the two forty two thousand it up that our column gives us the variance of the to sixty seven thousand that's in square units however. So we typically want the standard deviation. Let's take the standardized of these deviations which is going to be the seven six two zero zero zero square root, which is the eight seventy two.

And then we're going to compare that to the expected value, the mean or the average to then get to the coefficient of variation. So taking that divided by the one eight zero zero gives us three point four eight four nine about or about the point four eight five rounding three digits out. So now we can do our comparison. If we look at these two projects, we got the first one with the one thousand eight hundred expected value. The second one also has one thousand eight hundred expected values. So there even with regards to the expected value. So that then would lead you to believe that what you want to do is pick the one that has the least amount of risk, typically, because that would be more likely to to hit on, you know, you want the lower risk generally if the two expected values are the same.

And this one, the top one has the lower. Amount of risk, so the two things we take into consideration then being that expected value, that average value that we expect to have and then the level of the risk, obviously we would like, the higher expected value, the better. And the lower the risk, the better. So if you're in a situation where the expected value is the same and then the risk is different than we would typically want to pick the one with the lower risk, if you have the expected values that are different, then we might want to go to the higher expected value. If and when obviously the higher expected value had less risk, then we would want the higher expected value with less risk.

If the higher expected value had more risk, then we would have to be considering whether or not the added level of risk was justified in order to have that increased return. And we'd also have to be considering that kind of situation with regards to our risk tolerance level and the other types of investments that we have and what kind of investment we need to to fit into our overall type of risk assessment with our overall type of asset situation and finance situation, our whole accounting situation.

Expected Value & Net Present Value Even Yearly Cash Flows

We're going to look at a capital budget type of situation and apply our future forecasting kind of analysis to it. We'll also take a look at the present value calculation related to it. So a typical scenario when we have a capital budgeting type of situation is that we're going to imagine the initial cash outflow up front. In this case, that being fifteen thousand five fifty, so that we can then get cash inflows in the following year, we're going to imagine or in the following years, and because it's going to be affecting multiple years into the future, then we can apply our present value type of techniques, which would include the net present value and the internal rate of return. We're imagining here that we're going to put money into some type of equipment which will then have a five year life.

And we are also going to imagine that during those five years that the equipment will be in use. We're going to have either savings or cash inflows. We can have a cash benefit that will be even over that time period so that we can then think about our analysis. We'll do our analysis process to think about what the yearly cash flows will be and then use that to basically get to our expected value on a yearly basis. Note we're going to see a future problem in a future chapter, which will be slightly different. In other words, we could use this technique here to try to think about what the expected values will be in multiple different ways with these longer term capital budgeting types of projects.

For example, here we're going to imagine that we have the yearly cash flows being the same, and then we can basically figure out what we believe the possible yearly cash flows will be, then get to our expected value and then we can apply our net present value to that expected value for the five years. That's what we will do here. However, if the cash flows were not expected to be the same, then we could think about another type of method. We might then have to do, for example, present value calculations for each of our different scenarios so that we can then get to basically a bunch of different present value types of numbers that we can then apply our probabilities to. And we'll talk about that kind of method in a future chapter.

You can also think about a system where you might say, well, I'm going to use this kind of approach for each year within the capital budgeting process. So I might say, what are the cash flows going to be for year one after the equipment? I don't know. Let's do this type of approach and give some estimated answers and do our probability kind of assessment for a year one, then do the same thing for a year or two, same thing for year three and so on, getting an expected value for each of the years that the future cash flows will generate. And then we can use that to do our present value calculation. So we'll do those two kinds of formats. You might see those in future chapters right now.

The assumption being for this capital project, we have five years, the cash flows will be even coming in for those five years, and then we'll do our kind of probability analysis to figure out what those even cash flows would be. We've got the not good, the OK, good. Very good. Notice the names on the left hand side are not important. What's going to be important is what we believe the returns will be. So we believe that the not so good situation would be four thousand five hundred yearly for five years. OK, six thousand yearly for five years. Good. Eight thousand five hundred every year for five years and very good for ten thousand every year for the five years. Then we're going to assign our probabilities.

Where would this information come from? Possibly prior machinery that we have put in place and then and then projecting out into the future in terms of what the current economy basically looks like. This is a way to group our ideas so that we can get to an expected value so that we could basically move forward. Of course, looking into the future, we don't know. We're just making our best guess here. We're then going to take our probabilities. Got the 20 percent to 30 percent, the 30 percent and the 20 percent calculating those out. We got the four thousand five hundred times. Twenty percent is nine hundred thirty six thousand times. Thirty percent is going to be one thousand eight hundred. The eight thousand five hundred times thirty percent is the two thousand five hundred and fifty.

Then the ten thousand times the twenty percent is going to give us the two thousand, the two thousand. And then Of course the percentages have to add up to one hundred percent. That gives us an expected value for the yearly cash flow that we're assuming. That's what this is for, for the yearly cash flow for five years is seven thousand two hundred and fifty. Now that we have that expected cash flow, then we could go forward and say, let's do our present value calculation. This is where we have seen in basically a prior chapter where we focused a lot on these present value kinds of calculations for a capital budget. So if you want to spend more time on them, you could go to a prior chapter where we spend more time on that. The new thing here, Of course, is to get to this number.

So this number is what was kind of assumed in our prior chapters, right. In the prior chapters, we basically assumed that we knew or we had already come to what we believe the future cash flows would be. Using that information. We then calculated our net present value. Now, Of course, we're taking a step back here and saying it could take more detail. Of course. For us to figure out what we believe the future cash flows will be, and this is one method that we might take in order to think about what we believe the future cash flows would be. You could imagine these types of situations can be very difficult to organize if we're kind of trying to think about what things to invest in, because obviously many people might be involved. It's going to have a long term process that will be involved.

We're using estimates that will be involved and there might be people that have invested interest in one area or the other. So we want to do as much of a systematic approach as possible to be able to compare and contrast different methods and be able to explain where it is. We got to the numbers as much as possible so that we can have a good debate about what's the best place to put our money. So then we're going to get this information now. We're going to say the cost of capital is 14 percent. That's our discount rate. Let's calculate the net present value now with that 14 percent. That means that if the net present value is over, then zero, the 14 percent is included in it, which includes our return.

So if 14 percent is the hurdle rate, the cost of capital, if it's zero or above, then we've cleared the 14 percent and may then accept the project. So we're going to have year zero through five. We're going to put our cash flows. Note that we do have an annuity cash flow here. In essence, you might say, hey, this is an annuity. Why don't I do it with an annuity calculation? We will do that in a second here. But let's just do the standard present value kind of analysis. If these payments, Of course, were different every year, then we get this analysis would work in that format as well. So we're going to say the first outflow was that 15 five. That's going to be the outflow that we put down for the purchase of the equipment.

And then we figured that yearly inflows for the next five years to the life of the equipment are going to be even at the expected value of seven to 50. That's 7000 to 50. Then we can do our present value calculations. Remember that a few chapters back, we focused a lot on simply present value calculations. So you could do these with tables, you could do them with a formula, you could do them with Excel. We're going to focus on Excel here. If you want to look at them in different ways, then take a look at the present value calculation area. This is going to be the present value of one calculation. I'm going to do it on this first tab, even though we're at a time period zero so that we can then copy it down. If we were to do this in Excel, we can easily copy down the formula so we get the negative present value.

The rate is going to be the fourteen percent notice. It's an absolute reference to the sales by the dollar signs before the B and the Thirteen. That means when I copy it down, that cell will not move to the fourteen percent will be the same for each of these cells. The number of periods will be zero. Notice I referenced the cell to the right hand side instead of typing in zero so that I could copy that down and the relative cell will go down comma comma, because it's not an annuity, but the present value of one. And we will contrast that to an annuity calculation down below future values. The fifty five. The result is the same because we're at a time period zero. But if we copy that formula down, then in period one the seven thousand to fifty discounted at fourteen percent back one period or one year it will be six thousand three fifty.

And then in year two the seven thousand to fifty discounted at fourteen percent back two years will give us the five thousand five seventy nine the the seven thousand to fifty discounted back three years at fourteen percent gives us four thousand eight ninety for the seven thousand to fifty discounted at fourteen percent. Four years will give us the four thousand two ninety three and the seven thousand to fifty discounted at the fourteen percent. Five years will give us three thousand 765 65. Adding that up we get to the nine thousand three ninety because this is a positive number. That means we cleared the hurdle rate or cost of capital. A 14 percent might then consider taking on the project.

If we want to know what the actual rate was, possibly so we can compare it to another project, we can look at the internal rate of return, which could be calculated in Excel like this equals

IRR. And then just this series of numbers, negative outflow up front and then all the inflows. And that would then give us our value, which would be the thirty seven point one three percent. That's the rate at which if we did the net present value calculation using, we would end up with a result of zero and then we could do the same thing because it's an annuity. So just you might be saying, hey, you know, why don't I do an annuity calculation here for this portion since these payments are all the same? I noticed that in this situation, if you could do an annuity, you can always do a present value of one with these types of situations, this type of calculation, and sometimes you can do an annuity.

So in other words, you can always do a present value of one. And then sometimes if they're all the same, Of course, then you can do basically an annuity called. And in practice, it's actually nice to do the present value of once because it's easy to do and excel and you actually get a nice fuller picture of what's happening, happening in these capital projects. But in a book problem, they will often limit you because they might try to take away your calculator and whatnot. And so therefore they need to limit the calculations just for logistics purposes to get it done within a test type question time period. And so that's when they might do the annuity fight for time reasons. In that case, if you have excel, in other words, I think this format is actually better to explain your position or what's going on in the capital project in debate on it.

But the annuity calculation would be looking like this negative present value would pick up the rate, which again is that 14 percent. And then we'd say comma number of periods, which would be five years, and then comma the payment, which is going to be the annuity payment of the seven thousand to fifty for each of the periods that would give us the twenty four 890, that would be the inflow or present value of the inflows. If we compare that to the investment or outflow at time period zero for the purchase of the equipment 1500, we then get back to that nine thousand three ninety once again so we can also calculate this net present value that way. Also note that the annuity formulas, like I say, back in the prior chapters, when we talked about present value calculations, you can do that with a table. You could do that with formulas if you want to get more information on how to do that. Take a look at the prior chapters.

Expected Value & Coefficient of Variation Investment Options

We have our information up top going through the calculations down below. What can I imagine? We have two basic investment types of options that we're going to be comparing on a side by side basis, using the same kind of statistical type of analysis that we're trying to project into the future and put our thought process in the best way to do so as possible. And that means that we're going to be categorizing for each investment what we think the returns would be if it was in this case. But we have five categories. You don't really need the names for the categories on the left hand side. You need basically the numbers here, but sometimes it's useful to have the names of not good. OK, good.

Very good and extremely good. And then the numbers that would be representing that if that investment turned out in that way. And then Of course, there are probabilities that need to add up to 100 percent. Now, as we compare the two investments, what we want to get is going to be that bottom line return and then we can get our expected return. Clearly, the higher the better for the expected return. But then we also want to consider the amount of volatility or the amount of risk that might be involved, meaning that the amount that could be variations from what would be kind of like the mean expected value, the average here. And that's going to give us our amount of risk. And those are the two factors we typically want to take into consideration most with these kinds of calculations.

So with the first project notice, we broke them out, this time into five categories. There's no set amount of categories. Usually it's between like one and 10, usually like one in six or something like that is closer to it. And we're going to base it basically based on prior periods possibly, and what we think is going to happen in the future and then try to pick up what returns we think are most likely to be happening in those categories. Then we assign the probability of how likely we think those returns are going to be taking place. So we're going to say it goes from 600 to 650 to 800 to 950 to one thousand. If it's going from not so good to very good, then we're going to assign the probabilities in this case, the probabilities we assign evenly. Twenty, twenty, twenty, twenty, twenty.

Then the expected value is going to be the six hundred, twenty times the twenty percent or 120, the 650 times the twenty percent or one thirty. 800 times twenty percent or one sixty. The nine, fifty times the twenty percent or one ninety. The one thousand times the twenty percent, the two hundred. That gives us an expected value of eight hundred dollars. Option number two for, for the cash flows or our investments. This time we notice we have a different amount of categories. We have four categories. The two amounts of categories for our investments do not have to line up. They don't have to be the same. We're trying to think about the number of categories that would make more sense for us to break down our data in a way that we think is most applicable for that particular category so that we can get them to the expected value.

Notice here we have twenty eight values that should be expected values that are meaningless. So please disregard the twenty eight there. So we have the 650 at the not good, the OK 700, the good eight hundred and very good nine hundred. We have now assigned the probabilities that are going to be different this time. This is something we just came up with. This is something that we gave our best guess on. This is one way to structure our thought process, that being the forty percent, the twenty percent, the ten and then the thirty. So six, fifty times forty percent is going to give us the two sixty seven hundred times twenty percent gives us the 148 hundred times ten percent, the eighty, nine hundred times thirty percent, the 270.

Adding that up we get the expected value for the second one of the seven fifty. So of these two the first one would be better. Right. We got the 800 versus the 750. So if we just look at the expected value, you would think that given this, you know, spread of data that we had, the first option would be the best. Then we want to consider the amount of risk that would be involved as well. So now we want to go and say the second component is going to be the risk. We're back to investment one here. I won't recalculate it for us. There's the investment one we had before. That's the first one with the twenty, twenty, twenty, twenty investment. The probabilities. Let's calculate our risk now. So we're going to go through this calculation. We have the returns.

Same returns up top. We want to calculate the. Expected value, that's what we just did, that's the 800 dollars, then we're going to take the difference between the return of each return category and the expected return or average or mean of the 800. So the 600 miles, the 800, the 200, 650 minus the 800 to

150, these are negative 150, negative 200. And 800 minus 800 is zero. 950 minus the 800, 150. The one thousand minus the 800 200. Then we're going to take those differences and square them. I'll just do one calculation in the trusty calculator so we can see how it's done there. Make sure you get the squared button if you're going to need to be square and stuff on your trusty calculator, going to take a negative 200 and square it.

That's going to be 40000 40000. If we do the same thing for the negative 150, we get 22 five four zero, we get zero. That one I can do in my head. That one was amazing, 150 squared. We get the 2025 and the 200 squared, we get the 40000. Then we apply all the probabilities 20, 20, 20, 20, 20. And that's going to be our probabilities to get our end result at 40000 times. 20 percent is eight thousand twenty twenty five times the twenty percent four thousand five hundred the zero times the twenty percent zero. The twenty two five times twenty percent, four thousand five hundred. And the 40000 times that twenty percent gives us the eight thousand adding up the outer column then gives us the twenty five thousand. That's the variance.

It's in squared units. So typically we want the standard deviation. So we would typically take the square root of the variance taking the twenty five thousand and then square routine. Square root is this button. There's the button. I'm looking for the 158 eleven. And then we're going to compare it to the mean, which is kind of like the average or the expected value and dividing that that's what we calculated up top 800 divided by 800 is going to give us then the coefficient of variation. The point one nine seven six. This is not very useful in and of itself. If we only had one calculation, but when we compare it to the second one, then it can help us with our risk assessment. So we're going to go on down and say, well, let's do the second one here.

And we already did this part. So that's our expected value. You will recall from when we calculated it a while ago was 750. Hopefully you recall that. And now we're going to go and do the second component here. So we got our values, the 650 to the 900 expected value, which we calculated up top is the 750. The difference then being the 650 minus the 750, negative 100, 700, minus 750, 50 and the 800 minus the 750 is 50. The 900 minus the 750 is 150. The first two being negative, the second being positive. Then we will square each of them. I'll do the first one once again, just so we can check it out on the calculator. We've got 10000. Hold on a second. Calculators bounce it around, it's got a life of its own.

My calculator is running around negative and then we're going to square it so negative 100 squared is the 10000 that will do that. Same process for the negative 50 square is going to be the two thousand 550 square 2005 and 150 square 2025. And then we're going to use our probabilities, which you'll recall are the 40, 2010, 30. So there's our 40, 20, 10, 30, 10000 times 40 percent. Four thousand twenty five hundred times twenty percent is the five thousand two thousand five hundred times 10 percent to 50 twenty two thousand five hundred times 30 percent, six thousand seventy five zero. Adding up the outer column for the variance, we get to the eleven thousand five hundred. But those are squared units. So we typically take the standard def standard deviation that is.

And so we're going to take then the one one five zero zero and then we take the square root to give us the standard def. Of the one seven 24, comparing that then to the expected value, which you could think of as the mean or average divided by the 750, that 750 is what we calculate it up top here. And there it is, we get the what do we call it, the coefficient of variation point one four three zero about, and you could represent that as a percent or a decimal. So now if we do our comparisons, you'll recall that we had been the 800 that had the higher expected value for the invested one versus the 750 for the investment two. And it has now a higher risk to it as well.

So in that situation, the question would then be, is the higher expected value worth the added risk? That's going to be the typical kind of situation. Remember that it doesn't necessarily always happen that way. And so it's good to work multiple problems just to realize that it is. In other words, a lot of times people get the notion in their mind that added risk automatically means that there's a higher possible expected return. That's not always the case. You know, you can increase the risk and not have a higher expected return. However, it is the case that when you compare it to investments that are good investments, the higher you know, the higher risk on those types of investments could quite possibly result in a higher expected return.

The point being, you don't want to be taking on more risk just to take on more risk, assuming that it's going to have a higher expected return. You want to make sure that if you are taking on more risk, it's because it actually does have a higher expected return and that you measure it in that component.

See if you're risk averse or not risk averse or a common book question here would be asking whether someone be risk averse or not risk averse in the one willing to take take the chance for the higher return would be more more able to deal with what risk, whereas someone who was risk averse might choose the second option here. It also depends on where you are in terms of your total investment kind of portfolio or where your business is investing in terms of what types of investments would fit well within the risk assessment of your entire portfolio of investments.

Expected Value in Capital Budgeting Decision Uneven Payments

We're going have a similar kind of scenario with this capital budgeting type of decision, but it'll be a little bit different in how we apply our tools for this capital budgeting decision. So we're going to have to capital budgeting the kind of decisions that we want to be comparing and contrasting. The typical concept with the capital budgeting decision is we have the initial outflow going out up front and then we expect inflows to be happening in the future, four years into the future. The primary two tools that we would use then being those that take into consideration time, value of money, net present value calculations and the internal rate of return calculations we have going through those calculations, net present value and the internal rate of return in depth in a prior chapter.

So if you want to focus on them specifically, take a look at that. Now, we're going to be adding to it our analysis here for our probabilities and how we can basically work that into our analysis for our future projections. Now, in a prior chapter, we did a capital budgeting kind of process where we assumed that the future cash flows would all be the same. And we don't know. We didn't know exactly what the future cash flows would be, but we said, hey, we're going to invest in equipment, for example. It's going to have a five year life. So life is going to be the same for each of our estimates. And then we said the cash flows were going to be the same, but we don't know what it is.

And therefore, we used our analysis tool here with our probabilities that we've been working on in this chapter to figure out what the yearly cash flow would be getting then to the expected value, which we could then use in our net present value calculation. So that would work if we think the number of years would be the same for each of our kinds of scenarios within each individual investment. And if the cash flows would be even. But if we have different cash flows that we're expecting in each of our different scenarios and the length of the payment time is different, we think that possibly, you know, we might get paid for five years and then we might get paid for like 10 years. We don't know how long the future inflows will be beneficial from this primary investment.

And in that case we might have to take our three scenarios, we imagine are three scenarios and run a separate present value for each of the scenarios. So we won't actually do that here because it'll be kind of tedious and long to do that. So if you want to figure out how to do present value calculations, again, we've done those in prior chapters. But you can imagine a situation where now we cannot just. Take the expected value for all years and then do the net present value, but rather do the net present value first for our three scenarios, we imagine possibly one scenario, having year one cash flows being different from year to cash flows and maybe having, you know, five years of cash flow that we expect.

And then we could do our present value to get to the net present value using whatever discount rate would be applicable to do so. And then the second one, maybe we expect to get money back, you know, for four years or something like that in the future in that scenario. And the cash flows are different from year one to year two and so on. Then we can do our net present value calculation there and for scenario three. So in that situation, we might have to see the net present value calculations first. And then once we have the net present value, we're going to stay here from the initial inflows into the net present value of the future inflows. Then we can compare that to the cost in our case, this time being the one hundred thirty to get to the net present value.

So in essence, we calculated the net present value for our three alternatives here, and then we can assign the probabilities to that net present value calculation that gives us a lot more flexibility to basically be able to do whatever we want with the three scenarios within a particular investment plan. And again, a lot of times with these investments, we don't know how long they're going to be beneficial. We might say it might be benefiting us for five years or maybe it'll benefit us for 10 years. Maybe the equipment will last longer than the normal for whatever reason. And we want to run estimates in our options that will take that into consideration. What we could do if we do the net present value first and then we apply our percentages on the net present value calculation.

In this case, we got the inflows. The 190 minus the initial cost of 130 gives us the 60, the 200 miles to 137 to the ninety minus to 130 would give us 40. These would be our net present value possibilities then. Then our probabilities. 2060, twenty sixty thousand times twenty percent is twelve thousand seventy thousand times sixty percent. Forty two thousand forty two thousand negative times twenty percent. Negative eight thousand obviously again the percentages adding up to one hundred percent. So then there is the option to do the same kind of thing. We're going to say now we're going to compare it to another option, possibly comparing and contrasting which would be the better of the two.

This one, we have the initial down payment of the 200000, same kind of thing. We can have our three scenarios, but we're going to do the net present value calculation first so that we could run more varied scenarios for each of the three and then do our weighted average on the net present value calculation. So these would be our cash flows that we're assuming for the three, the four hundred, the three, ten and the fifty. The cost is two hundred across the board. So the net present value for the first one would be the 400 miles, 200 or 200, then the second three. Ten minus the 200000 or the 110. Third one 50000 minus the 200000 is the negative. One hundred and fifty probabilities assigned 50 percent, 20 percent, 30 percent. Then we're going to say the first one is the two hundred thousand times the fifty percent. One hundred thousand.

One ten thousand times twenty percent. Twenty two thousand and one fifty thousand negative times 30 percent. Forty five for an expected value of seventy seven thousand. This Of course adds up to one hundred. Now we can compare these expected values to forty six thousand to seventy seven thousand and do that type of analysis between these two. Now there are some limitations here, Of course, because when we do these net present value calculations, we're usually clearing over the cost of capital. So there could be some situations where if the amount of investments is substantially different, we want to make sure that we're careful on the comparison between these two items.

But you can see how this is a method that we can use to apply our statistical kind of analysis tool and still do some more complex scenarios on the three scenarios per investment. So that's another way that we can apply this kind of scenario. Also another way that we'll take a look at in a future chapter to apply this type of probability scenario to a capital budgeting situation would simply be to then have a share each year of the capital budgeting. So let's say we have one investment project that has five years and we don't know what the actual inflows will be per year. We might want to dive deeper into what we think the inflow will be for year one versus year or two versus year three. And so we might run scenarios like this for each of the years of the five years of the capital investment to get to. Better drill down on what we believe the actual inflows will be for each capital investment, so we might take a look at a problem like that in the future.

Expected Value for Multiple Years & NPV

Closing the icon information up top is going to go through the calculations down below. We're going to continue on with the idea of a capital budgeting type of process here and our idea of trying to organize our data in this kind of statistical type of way so that we can make a good judgment into the future, a way to organize our thoughts as we make our projections. So the typical capital project, you'll remember, you'll recall, will typically include an outflow up front money going out so that we have benefits in future years, typically then having an impact in future years. The primary tools that we usually use to calculate them are the present value tools of the net present value and the internal rate of return.

We focused a lot on those calculations in prior chapters now. And so you go back there if you want to, to focus on that. Now, we're going to add the added detail of this type of analysis for this percentage type of analysis to make projections into the future. Now, we've done this a few different ways for these longer term projects. Now how we can apply, in other words, this percentage kind of allocation. One practice problem we did a couple problems ago on these capital budgets would be a situation where we think, for example, we have one piece of equipment that we're putting out up front, and then we think that it's going to have five years return or some set amount of years of return where the inflows will be the same for each year.

In that case, what we did is we used our statistical kind of category analysis to figure out what we believe the cash flow might be under different kinds of scenarios, different kinds of projections. And then we got our expected value based on that, that we then apply the net present value calculation to. That's one way you can then work this thought process into the capital budgeting decision. We also thought about a situation where it might be somewhat more complex than a situation where you do not even have cash flows. And one way you could still work in this thought process is possibly to then work out each of the three scenarios that you might take for the entire life of the capital project under three different scenarios, allowing you a lot more diversification and then take those net present values and then allocate them into our kind of thought process here to get our expected net present value.

That's another method that can be used. This is the third method that we're using that we can apply to this cash flow or budgeting type of process. In this case, we might say, let's take one capital budgeting process and remember the assumptions that we typically make with a capital budgeting process in order to figure out the net present value or what's going to be the initial outflow. That's something that's usually given that we know that we can kind of figure that to a pretty high degree of accuracy, but we don't know the inflows. That's, Of course, a projection into the future. And if you're talking about more complex types of projects that are happening in the future, the inflows that are coming back are really just a guess.

And they could be substantially different from year one year to year three. If you're talking three years out, it could be substantially different what's going to happen in year five versus year one. And so therefore, you might try to apply this kind of statistical concept per year to try to think about how much your actual cash flows will be for each of the years to come up with different cash flows basically each year and then apply your net present value. So that's going to be this method we'll take a look at here. So, for example, here we're going to add it even a little bit more difficult, a little bit more complicated, and that it's not going to be, we're not going to have cash flows coming back each year. So we're going to get cash flows coming back after one year.

And then we're going to say after three years and after nine years, just to add a little bit more of a complexity in it. But just realize, even if you got cash flows back every year, you can apply the same kind of concept and it might be applicable to do so if it's complex in terms of how much money you're going to get back each year. So we might say for year one, for example, we could say low average, high. Remember that the number of categories don't really matter. The names don't really matter. The numbers matter, but usually it's about one to five. Categories, and then we will apply how much we might get if it was low average or high based on past experience and our projections into the future, if it was low.

We're saying 300 four years, one average, 800 high one thousand, then we'll apply our percentages. This is our best guess. Again, to try to think about how likely it would be for these outcomes to come into play. So low is going to be the 40 percent average, 20 and high at the 40. Those percentages have to add up, Of course, to 100 percent, 300 times. The 40 percent is one twenty eight hundred times. Twenty percent is one sixty one thousand times. 40 percent is 400. 120 to 160 to 400. That adds up to the 680. So the expected value of year one of this extended project, we're going to say, is 680. Then, Of course, as we do the net present value, we can use that number to do our discounting back to the net present value when we do our net present value, which we will see shortly. And then we're going to say there was no income in year two.

We're going to project that it's an unusual stream of income coming back. Right. And then in year three, we're going to get income. We're staying low advertised. So we're thinking five hundred, eight hundred and one thousand two hundred percent, the thirty, forty thirty on the percent. So the five hundred times the thirty percent, one fifty, eight hundred times the 40 percent is going to be 320. The one thousand two hundred times thirty percent is going to be the 360. The percentages Of course add up to one hundred percent and then the totals now add up to the eight thirty. So for year three now we're guessing then we have an expected value.

Our best guess based on this type of analysis is eight thirty for the expected value there, which once again we can present value or use that as part of our present value calculation. And then year nine, once again, we're assuming that it's a weird cash flow situation. We're not getting any more cash flow back until year nine, where we have then low average high four hundred, eight hundred and nine hundred forty two thousand forty on the breakouts of four hundred times forty one sixty eight hundred times twenty one sixty. And then the 900 times to forty or the 360 the the totals adding up to one hundred percent on the percentage that gives us the six hundred and eighty. So the one that's at nine years out, we think that the value that we're expecting to receive is the 980.

So once we have that, once we've analyzed all the cash inflows basically on a one by one process using this analysis, then we can use that to do our net present value type of calculation. Before we do note, we're going to do the other kind of statistical for the coefficient of variation here. So the coefficient of variation, calculation for the three of them just to practice with that as well. You can do that basically on a year by year basis. That can give you some more detail if you were to compare these and it also just gives us good practice to work through these types of problems. So we're going to say for year one, if we had our same returns here, the 300, the 800, the one thousand. And I'll go through this a little bit more quickly because we have seen these in the past. The expected value or average is going to be the 680 of the 680, the 680 that we calculated up top.

The difference, the three hundred minus the 680 is a negative three eighty eight hundred minus 680 is the one twenty one thousand, minus 680 is the 320. Then we square these items. And if you want to see this more slowly going through, you can take a look at some prior chapters where we spent a little bit more time on these. We'll just do it a little bit faster here. We got 380 negatives squared. Forty four for 120 squared is the fourteen for 320 squared is going to be the one or two for probabilities then are the next item. That's going to be the 420 forty. The one forty four. Four times forty percent is fifty seven. Seven sixty. The fourteen, four times the twenty percent is the two thousand eight eighty and the one or two four times the forty percent forty thousand nine sixty.

Adding up the outer column gives us the variance of the one oh one six hundred. Then we would take the square root of that to get the standard deviation. Three eighteen seven seventy five. Then we divide by the expected value which is the number we calculated up top three eighteen point seventy five divided by the 680 gives us the coefficient of variation that point for six nine. Let's do it then. For year three we have then the return up top, the 500, the 800, the one thousand two expected values calculated at the eight thirty. The differences then here. Five hundred minus the three eighty. The negative three thirty eight hundred minus the eight thirty. The negative thirty one thousand two hundred minus to eight thirty to three seventy.

We square those negative three thirty squared one zero eight nine hundred negative thirty squared 900. The three seventy squared one thirty seven nine apply and then the probabilities at the thirty forty thirty thirty forty thirty gives us then our one two eight nine times thirty. Thirty two six seven seventy nine hundred times, 40 percent, the three sixty one three six, nine times the 30 percent, the forty one seventy, adding those up gives us the variance. The seventy four, one hundred taking the square root standard deviation to seventy to twenty one. Comparing that dividing by the eight thirty which is the expected value, average or mean gives us the coefficient of variation. Point three two eight three two eight. One more time for year nine.

We're going to say the return, the returns are the four hundred, the eight hundred, the nine hundred four eight nine. The expected value we calculated at the six eighty the difference to four hundred minus the 680 negative to eighty. The eight hundred minus the six eighty. The one twenty. The nine hundred minus the 680. The two twenty the negative two eighty squared seventy eight for one twenty squared fourteen four to twenty squared forty eight for probabilities then forty two forty forty two forty three seventy eight. Four hundred times the forty percent gives the thirty one six three sixty the fourteen four times the twenty percent gives the two thousand eighty eighty the forty eight thousand four hundred times the forty percent gives the nineteen 360.

Adding those up gives us the variance. The fifty three six hundred standard deviation square root of that is two thirty one fifty two. Then we take that compared to the expected value divided by in other words the expected value of the six eighty to get the coefficient of variation the point three four zero. So now we'll go to, we'll go to the kind of a new thing here, which is to do the present value calculation. So you'll recall we have the expected value in year one, the six eighty and then the eight thirty. And then and that was in year three. And then in year nine, we had six eighty. And so we could do this in two different ways. We can do it the easy way where we're not going to have every year because some years we didn't have cash inflows or we can list off all the inflows here. So let's do it the short way first.

So the way I would basically set this up in Excel is to set our table from periods zero. And usually I would go zero down to how many years there are. But now I'm only going to include the years that have activity in them. So year zero, one, three and nine, these are going to be important because I'm going to use them as cell references. If I were to calculate these using Excel the first period zero was the outflow, which we're saying was one thousand four hundred. Then we'll apply the present value, the present value calculation to the outflow that happened at period zero then will have no impact, meaning that the amount will be the same. But in Excel we can copy that down.

Also note that if you want to know how to do this, present value calculations multiple ways, like with a table or with formulas. Take a look at some prior chapters where we spend more time on that. We'll do that more quickly here. Just referencing how we would do it in Excel. So we'd say in Excel we take the negative present value, the rate, the rate. I'm picking up the sale, the fifteenth. It's going to be an absolute reference by dollar sign before the C and the eight. So if I copy it down, I can copy it down easily and not have that cell reference move comma. And then we have the number of periods which is zero. Instead of typing it in there, I'm referring to this so.

So once again it will copy down for us and make our life easier, comma, comma. And then we have the future value which is that one thousand four hundred. The result is the same because we're at period zero and then that period one. If we copy this down we would take the six eighty and take that back for one year. Let's just get rid of all these. We see that's going to be period one and period three. We're going to bring that back one year. So the negative present value is going to be the rate of the same cell here, which is that fifteen percent absolute reference comma number of periods, which is now going to be one. So it's picking up this one here instead of a hard code in it, the cell goes down from two to three and then comma, comma, future values that 680. So we discount it back, giving us the five ninety one.

Now if I copied the cell reference down, you'll note that this cell right here, which represents the number of periods, would copy down from this one to three because we skipped period two. So that's why this column is helpful over here. So in other words, if we discounted the eight thirty, which we got from this reference, this calculation is our expected value. Is this eight thirty? And we discount it back three years using the discount rate of the fifteen percent, we get the five forty six and then your nine. We're saying nothing happened until year nine where we had the expected value of the 680. So now we're going to take year nine, year three. But it was eight thirty three. Was the eight thirty discounted.

Back three years at 15 percent gives us 546, your nine is the 680, which we're going to discount back nine years at 15 percent to give us the 193. Then if we sum these up, we get a negative 70. That means we haven't cleared the hurdle rate or the discount rate. So we might not take on the project based on that because we haven't cleared the 15 percent. If it was zero or above, you'll recall that might be something that we would then take on. That's the general rule for the net present value that you could set up the table that looks like this as well. You might just have years one through nine, even though many years are zero and say at period zero, we have the 1400 negative outflow and then the 680 period one.

That's from our expected value. Nothing happened in year two, year three, the 830 that came from our expected calculation over here, nothing happens from four to eight. And then period nine we have the 680 and then we can simply copy down. This would be more tedious to do if we were to do this in a book problem, because it would take more calculations if you take longer to list this out. But if you do it in Excel, it's really easy to do. You'd have the same formula up top and then you could simply copy that formula down and it would be fine if it was zero, it would be fine. And you can calculate this quite easily and you might be able to show people pictorially. It might make it a little bit more clear about the strangeness of the project. Right.

To show that we have all these years that we have, we expect no inflows that are going to be happening. And the inflows on one year out, three years out and the nine years out. Same result, though. We got one year out. We discount the 680 back one year at the 15 percent to get the five 91, the one that four, three years out was the 830. We're going to discount it back for three years at fifteen percent to get the five. Forty six and the six eighty nine years back that we calculate nine years back at fifteen percent for the one ninety three to total up to that seventy negative once again below zero, therefore not taking into consideration or not clearing the 15 percent rate. And so we may not take on the project in that case.

So as we go through the different kinds of ways and angles, you can look at these projected problems, hopefully, hopefully you get some idea of the complexity that goes into the decision making that would be involved as you're kind of projecting out into the future to to make these decisions. There's no set process because it's not a done thing. We're using the best tools we can in order to make predictions about the future and the best decisions we can.

Standard Deviation, Variance, & Coefficient of Variation

You can find a lot of information about this out on the Internet and whatnot on YouTube and other places as well, just in terms of math theory. And you can look up things like the standard deviation, the variance and the coefficient of variation. Then we're going to take those tools and we'll apply them in more of a corporate finance type of setting in the future problems. So a quick recap on some of these statistical kinds of numbers. We have the population mean, which is the average of the population data points, the variance, which is the disbursement of a set of data points around the mean.

So these are common types of things we want to do with a data set, meaning first we often calculate the mean or the average to find that middle point. Remember, the mean is basically the average, something like the median would be the middle point in the data range of the data set. But we're usually thinking first about the average and average being kind of around the middle. Typically, we're taking the average and then we want to think about basically the dispersement or variance of the data around that average point. How widely dispersed are the data points around? Basically the meaning.

So if we were to take a simple dataset just like one through five, if we just count up one to five, typical things we might do to this data set in order to get a better understanding of it would be maybe one sum it up, get the total of it. That's going to be fifteen in this case. Then we might compare that then to the pop to the number of components in the population, a population size. This one obviously has five components: one, two, three, four or five. So we can then say account. I'm going to count those up using a count formula. So is the fancy way to count them equals count in Excel? So we'll count these up and they'll just take the units or the cells with units and then we have the five there.

Now if we divide that out, the total divided by the population size 15 over five, we then get the AMIEN or the average, which in this case would be three. That's one of the first things that would basically be done here. Now, note, the mean is kind of the same as the median in this case. Remember, the median is when you take basically the middle number, you pick up the middle one, which sometimes can give you a different data set to spend depending on the type of data that you have. But normally we're going to start off with that meaning here. Right. And the calculation you might see written like this. It's going to be the calculation of the sum of the data points divided by the number of points, which is going to be the population size. Now, then the next thing we might want to get is the variance.

So now that we have the mean, we want to think about how widely dispersed the data points are around that center, because that if we're trying to make projections into the future, trying to see what the actual population is, then we're going to we're going to want to basically or get a characteristic of what that population is. We want to think about how spread out it is from that, what we kind of think about the center point. So we could do a formula like this to start off the population variance, which would be the sum of each data point, minus the mean or average that we just calculated in this data set to the power of two squared, in other words, divided by the population size or end.

So if we were to run that out for our one through five data set, it would simply look like one minus three squared, plus two minus three squared plus three minus three squared plus four, minus three squared plus five minus three squared. So notice what's happening here when we take this number minus the mean of each number in our data set, minus the mean, the closer it is to the mean, the smaller the number that we're going to have as a result. So the closer it is to the mean average, the smaller the number that we're going to have as a result of these items. Also note that here, the one minus three, you would then result in a negative number, whereas if you had the four minus three, you'd have the positive number by a square in each of them.

That's going to result in one of them all becoming positive. So now we're having positive numbers because we're dealing with distance here. So that's one thing that we kind of want and it'll amplify the result due to it being squared here. So let's do this with a mathematical kind of calculation here in Excel. It would typically be mapped out something. Like this, so let's do it in Excel, same data set, which is going to be one through five, we're just going to say equals that one through the five. So we'll bring that down to five and then we'll compare that to the mean or the average. Let's calculate it again. This time, let's use a formula to do it. This is going to be equal to the average average and double click on this data set of numbers one through five. That's going to give us three, which we see here as well.

Now, every other cell, I'm going to say equals that three to bring it on down instead of doing the average five times. And then I can drag that down so every cell equals the one above it. That sometimes is an easy way to populate your data set in Excel. And then the difference here will take the difference here. And now we're basically doing the one minus three. We're taking the difference of each one now in a vertical fashion. So one minus three would obviously be negative to two. Minus three is going to be negative one three minus three will Of course be zero four. Minus three is going to be one and five minus three is going to be two. Now, if I add up this data set, Of course, because we have the negatives and positives around the mean and we're going to get zero in this case.

So what we want to do then, these negative numbers, when we square it will basically go away because we're talking about distance from the average rate. We're talking about different distances from the middle here. So we want these to basically be positive, different differences. And when we square it, it'll make it kind of amplify the differences as well. So let's do that. That's, Of course, bringing it to the power up top for each of these. So now we would get the result of all these and then we'll sum them up, which would be adding them up in our formula. So this will be the two, I'm going to say shift six for the carrot and then two. Right.

So then I'm going to say this is going to be the negative one cell shift six, and then I'm going to say two. And so now we've got obviously a positive number and it's four now. And then this is going to be positive. One, this will be this one shift six and two, which is zero. This is going to be one shift six and two. We have one. And this is going to be to shift six carats and two and so that we have four. So now we have a positive set of numbers. If I sum these up, then I'm going to sum these up and there we have it. And this is going to be our total recall total. All right. And then we're going to take the population size here. So taking the population size, which once again, we can count them by saying equals count.

So I'm just counting the number of items in the population now, which are five. Right. There would be some of these or the count of those, which would be the five items. And if I underline that now we divide it by the five here, that's going to give us our population variance. Population variance, then is the ten divided by five? So that can be a useful number. But note that we had to square it. So oftentimes then the next step is to go to the standard deviation, which is kind of removing the squared portion. Right. The squared helped us to basically amplify the number and get to basically positive numbers up top. So then the standard deviation is simply going to take that population variance and take the square root of it, kind of removing the square component. Right. So now we're going to say this and we can do this with a formula.

This would be the square root. Square askew. Square root would be in Excel of this too. And then enter. I'm going to basically add some decimals there and there we have that. So we just took the square root of the population variance that gives us then our standard deviation. Now if we compare that to the mean, so the mean or the average we can say mean or the average, then we're going to say this is going to be the mean of the average, which we had was three. Before that, we've calculated a couple of different ways. And that will then get us to the coefficient of variation, coefficient of variation being equal to the one point four one four two one divided by the three by the mean giving us. And then I'm going to add some decimals.

Sometimes this will be represented in a decimal format or sometimes in a percent format. Now note that the standard deviation is going to be basically in the units of the items that we're measuring in. So if it was dollars, we're talking basically in dollars. But if we have the coefficient of variation, that's going to be compared. And if we have two different data sets, it actually compares the variation a little bit more easily. So we can have different data sets that have a similar dispersion, but they have different dollar amounts. And this coefficient of variance will make it easier to see what that dispersion will be as we compare the two different data sets that will become more apparent as we go through practice problems in the future and do the. Harrison's on the side by side comparison.

Now let's do some of these with the formulas on the left hand side. So if I was just to do this quick hand on the formulas, we can say, OK, the average or the mean we can do this equals the average in Excel. We call it the average in Excel. And we would then just take this sum of data as we did before, or the average of them, that data range. And that would give us then the three the standard deviation we can take, the standard deviation. This equals the standard S t and then we have the EDV for the population or the sample notice. It could be a slight difference for the population or the sample. We're going to be using a population sample , meaning you don't have all the data. It's a sample of the data and the population mean and we have a full dataset that we're taking a look at.

So we're going to take the standard deviation of P. We could sum up this data set again and then we get to one. We can then add some decimals, adding some decimals, then there would get to that one point for one and so on that we have over here. And then we have the variance, which we can get to by saying this equals the variance variance. And we're going to say of the population, again, variance of the population picking up, then one through five and inter. And so there we have our two. So that's going to be our population variance. And then the coefficient of variation. Once we have these two numbers, we can then take the one point four, one four and so on, standard deviation divided by the mean or average, which would be three.

And then we can add some decimals to that. And then we get back to this point four seven. So let's think about it again. Now, let's take a look at this again. With two datasets side by side, they're going to be similar in nature, but they're going to have different dollar amounts or diffcrent amounts that will be included. You can consider them as dollar amounts. So we have the first data set, one, two, three, three, five, six, seven, eight, nine and 11. And the second data set being 20, 40, 60, 60, 100, 120, 140, 160, 180 and 220. Now you can see the second data set is derived by simply taking the first data set times 20. So you'll have a similar kind of characteristic in terms of we're just amplifying it by twenty dollars.

So when we think about the comparison of these data sets, you would think they would have things in common, even though we have different total amounts involved. So if you're thinking about dollar amounts, for example, and you were trying to compare two different data sets, you might want to know about the outline of the data set and the variance of the data set. Even though you're talking about two data sets with two different dollar amounts, the similarities could basically tell you something about possibly those data sets. So let's go ahead and do these calculations again. So we'll do a similar type of process. Let's put our data set one into this first table.

I'm just going to say one and then I'll copy this down till we get to the end of the data set, which was eleven. And so there we have that. Let's calculate the mean or the average. I'm going to say this is the average double click on that, summing up the data set and then entering. And so we have the average. Let's add some decimals numbers, a couple of decimals. Then I'm going to go underneath it and just say equals to sell above it. And I'll copy that down a little bit and then I'll copy that down. So all cells will equal the one above it, but still make it a little bit easy to calculate, oftentimes useful tools.

No group. Let's add a couple of decimals there. So there we have that and then we can take a look at the difference. So first we have the one minus the one point five. Let's go ahead and add decimals here to all these first numbers of groups. Add a couple of decimals. So negative 4.5. And then if we had the second piece of data minus the 5.5, negative three point five three minus five point five, negative 2.5, three minus 5.5, negative two point five five minus five point five, negative point five six minus five point five point five. We got seven minus five point five, one point five eight minus five point five 2.5 nine minus five point five, three point five and eleven minus five point five giving us the 5.5. So now we're going to square all these. We'll take each data set and square it.

So this equals the data set carrott to square in it. I'm going to copy this one down. Let's go ahead and put our cursor on it and autofill that on down and then we'll add a couple of decimals. No group, add a couple of decimals there. So the difference column, because we have the positive and negative numbers, is not going to give us, you know, the distance that we would basically like as much because it has those negative numbers. So when we squared it, you could see we have all positive numbers here. If I was to sum that up equals the sum of these items, that's going to give us the ninety seven. Let's add some decimals, add some decimals to this whole thing here.

So I have one at a time throughout the whole thing together. And then we'll take a look at the population size so the population puts them underlines under these two font groups and underline population size, we just count the items in the population. So I'm going to use the trusty count function this time, count when I count these items from here to here and then enter and that it's ten. One, two, three, four, five, six, seven, eight, nine, 10. That's all it did. And there's the ten. We're going to say let's underline that, underline their population variance. Then the population variance is going to be equal to the ninety six point five divided by the ten. So there we have nine points and six five.

Let's calculate then the standard deviation on it, which would simply be the square root of that. So this is like the squared values that we want to bring back. So and if this was done, this would be like in square dollars, right? We want to bring it back to the unit. So I'm going to say this is going to be equal squared. The square root of that squared, the square root of the nine point sixty five, that's going to give us the three point one one standard deviation, if we compare that to the mean or the average, which we calculated to be, you'll recall the five point five underlining that by going to the group and underline, that'll give us the coefficient of variation for the population, which is going to be equal to the standard deviation divided by the mean.

And that's going to give us that five point five six. Now, let's see if we compare this. Let's put a total here. Let's compare this to data set two. So let's do a similar kind of thing with data set to picking up the data and copy that on down. I'm going to select the whole thing this time and add some decimals before we even start this time. No group adds a couple of decimals, then will autofill that down to the ten components for all of our data. Let's calculate the mean, which is going to be the average equals average average of this data set and enter. I'm going to say this equals the one above it and then copy that down. We'll put our cursor on that Phil handle and copy it down. So there's the one ten all the way down.

Then we'll do the subtraction, subtracting it out. So the T minus the one ten negative ninety forty minus to one ten negative seventy sixty minutes to one ten negative fifty sixty minus to one ten negative 56. Similar trend that we have here with regards to the distance from the mean, meaning the spread of the data from kind of like the center point or mean that we would calculate. So we'd have that one hundred minus the one ten. We've got 120 minus one ten. We've got 140 minus the one ten. We've got the 160 minus to 110, the 180 minus to one ten. And finally the 220 minus the one ten. So again, you can see some similarities here with this disbursement of differences to this distortion of differences, even though we have, Of course, different dollar amounts that are involved. Now, we're going to remove the negative numbers by squaring it.

And this will amplify the difference as well. So we're going to say this is going to be equal to this number. I'm going to say shift six to the power of two, squaring it. Let's copy that all the way down. So if we copy that all the way down there, we have it making the cell a little bit larger because that last one is a big number. Give it some room. It's a big guy group and underlined. And then we got the population size. So this is going to be the total. We'll just pull the same over here. Population size, the size of the population. Then it's going to be, let's do the total. First total is going to be the sum of these so that we got the 3600 population size. Let's do the count equals the count. So we'll take the count of and we're going to pick up these numbers.

It's just going to count them out. There'll be ten of them again, underline, font, group and underline. And that'll give us the population variation, population variation, which is going to be equal to the thirty eight six divided by the ten. That's going to be three thousand eight sixty. So that's the population variation. And then we're going to take a look at the standard deviation, standard deviation. So notice again these to these population variations because they're amplified now because we squared them aren't as comparable. They're not in there like squared units. If they were, they'd be in like square dollars. So now we're going to basically take the standard deviation, the square root, in other words, of the population variance, which will be equal to the square root as square root of the cells, which is square root.

And that'll give us the 62 thirteen sixty two thirteen on the standard deviation. Now these two numbers are now in dollars, but they're still not very comparable. Right. I would like to be able to see something that shows that the variation is somewhat the same basically between the two and we can't really see that in the standard deviation here. So let's take a look at the coefficient of coefficient of variation by then picking up the mean, the mean which we calculated to be equal to one hundred and ten. Underline that font group and underline and that'll give us then the coefficient of variation being the 62 thirteen divided by the one ten. And so there's the fifty point five six. So notice that these two give us a better kind of idea.

If we're comparing two different data sets about the disbursement of the data around that kind of center point or the average point, and don't get the center point of the mean mixed up with the median. But this means the average point that we're talking about, which usually people can. As the center point or the average of the data and then the disbursement of the data around, basically that average can be nicely seen here with the point five, six, even though, again, we're talking about different amounts. If you're thinking about financial type of matters, we might be talking about different data sets that have different dollar amounts that are involved, but have a similar disbursement once again around the meet.

Now, you could do that again with the calculations down below. Let's try to use Excel and try to do this without a full table. Now, it's really useful to do the full tables, by the way, because that gives you a much better understanding about what's happening. And just looking at the data, because remember, when you're looking at these data sets, you're trying to get a different perspective about the data sets that tells you something about them that might be useful to whatever you're trying to do. So actually mapping out the data sets in this format can give you a visual look at what these data sets are doing. I mean, just by looking at these two data sets, we could start to see if there's something similar about these two, right? We could start to pick things up just by doing the calculation.

So it's worthwhile to do that. That's what statistics is basically doing. No one stat oftentimes when you're looking at a data set, can tell you everything you need to know. The average doesn't tell you everything you need to know. That's why people can lie about numbers, right? Because they use one data set and they build a whole story around one small piece of truth and one small piece of truth isn't the whole story. You've got one small piece of truth and a bunch of lies. Right? What you want to do is look at it from many angles so that you can try to peer in as many angles of truth that you can find and put together a story that actually is as close to the truth as you can get. Right. So and so if we have over here, we could do this with the calculations with Excel, though.

So the average would be the average and this would be like the mean or the average. So the calculation Excel is the average table will take the average of these 5.5 data sets to you if we took the average. So equals average double clicking on that in just select the data like you would with the sum function. There we have it. If we take the standard deviation, that's going to be this I our type in S-T. And then you got the standard deviation of the P or S. Now, these could come up to slightly different results. If you want to get more research on those different results, then you can look this stuff up. There's a lot of great math, just straight math kind of calculations.

These things are often used when you're taking a look at sample sizes and things like that. But we're going to use the population here as if we have the whole population and we're going to be summing up then or not summing up, but taking the data kind of similar to what you would do into some formula of this range of cells that we have. Let's do it again. This is going to be equal to the ESTIE standard deviation of these items, picking up these numbers. All right, and then we have the variance, the variance is going to be equal to the V.A. are so very variance. Once again, we have the population versus the sample. I'm going to take the population being consistent here, picking up the numbers on this one for a data set, one similar kind of format, and then the variance P picking up the numbers for this data set. And so there we have it.

We could see these numbers lining up. We got the five the five point five, five point five, the three point one one three point one one, the nine point sixty five, the nine point sixty five. And then the coefficient of variation being equal to then the mean divided by the standard. I'm sorry. Hold on a second. Equals the standard deviation divided by the mean so that we got the point five, six doing it over here, the standard deviation divided by the mean. So we got once more standard deviation divided by the mean. So there we got point five six.

OK, so there's the point. Five, six point five six here and then the 110, Of course, matching the 110 in the second data set the 62 13 standard deviation, matching out the three eight six zero variance matching out here. And then the point, five six, Of course, bottom line number for the coefficient of variation. So get an idea of these kinds of things. Is that really, really useful tools to analyze data sets? They're used all the time and different kinds of settings, and they become useful and will take some of these tools and apply them out to situations, possibly forecasting prediction types of situations in future chapters.

Expected Value, Standard Deviation, & Coefficient of Variation

We're going to add we're going to imagine we have an advertising campaign that's going to be taking place. And once you get the concept of this, you can start to apply to many types of things to try to get more of a systematic approach as you're projecting things out into the future. So we're going to see the possibilities. We're going to break those out into some possibilities and then assign probabilities to those possibilities. So we're going to say that we have a low outcome, average outcome or very high outcome. And then we're going to basically assign in this case what would happen in a quantitative measure of those different outcomes. In this case, we're talking about unit sales.

So we're going to imagine we sell 650 units at the low outcome, 750, average high 900, and then very high at the one thousand. So once we have our probabilities and notes, again, this is all estimates, Of course, into the future. So if we're talking about our advertising campaigns, we would have to look into the past and think about what has happened in prior advertising, possibly get some averages from it. And possibly these are coming from our prior campaigns in terms of low average, high and very high. Then we could basically group our categories and then we'd have to come up with probabilities. Now, again, how would you possibly know what the probabilities are? You have to go to the past depending on the type of data set that you're looking at.

So you'd have to come up with the probabilities, possibly looking at past advertising campaigns, seeing what has happened then and then thinking about the current scenario, the current economic situation, and then try to assign probabilities that you think the campaign will be average, low, high or very high. And then we're going to calculate our expected return here. So obviously, the probabilities that we would have to assign would need to add up to one hundred percent. So this could be a way for us to kind of break down our thinking into the future. It can be a little bit abstract when we think about the future and we have nothing really to go on.

It could be useful to break down our data based on past information and the estimates into the future, into some kind of categories or a range of ways that things could turn out and then give our probabilities as to how likely those things might turn out again based on past data. But, Of course, taking into consideration changes in the future. And that could be a more systematic way for us to kind of think about what might happen. So if we take our totals here, we're going to say the 650 times the 20 percent then has a one thirty one thirty, the 750 times the 20 percent, the 900 times the 30 percent and the one thousand times the 300 percent.

So then if we were to add those up, we get our total expected value, which would then be 850. So we're going to say that basically our expected value then is going to be then the 850 in this case. Now to break this down and show how we're kind of putting this into our statistical type of analysis. Let's imagine then that these outcomes, let's put them into a series of numbers, a set of numbers that have 10, 10 numbers to them just so we could see how the statistical kind of analysis works in a normal number set. And then we'll do the same thing, applying it in a slightly different kind of way to calculate the standard deviation and the coefficient of variance.

So let's imagine this data set over here. We're saying that 650 will be the outcome 20 percent of the time. 750 would be the outcome, 20 percent of time, 930 and one one thousand thirty percent of the time. So let's just imagine then that we have the 10 outcomes that came out in that in that in that weather in other words, I'm just going to have a list of numbers. I'm going to say that 650 equals to 650. And that's going to happen out of ten times. It'll happen twice, 20 percent of the time. And then we're going to say that the 750 over here is going to happen twice. I'm going to say it equals the one above it. That's going to be 20 percent of the time. And then the night 900, we think out of ten would happen three times. And then the 1000 we're thinking out of ten, 30 percent would happen three times.

So this set of ten numbers, then it's kind of reflecting our probabilities here. We got 20 percent, two out of 10, 20 percent. Two out of 10, three out of 10, 30 percent and three out of 10 the 30 percent for the very high. So if we take a look at that normal kind of data set of numbers, the natural thing to do then would be to say total will total this thing up equals the sum of this data set that would then give us if we underline that font, we're going to say that some would be the eight thousand five hundred. We can then take the mean or the average, which would be equal to the average double clicking the average, which would be all of these, or it would be the eight thousand five hundred divided by the number of items the population, which was 10.

And that would give us in the 850, I'm going to say equals and select the eight fifty above it and then just simply autofill that down. So I'm going to put the same mean all the way down the average number. Then we can look at the difference. Right. The difference would be the 650 minus the 850. The difference here would be the 650 minus the 850. Again, we have the 750 minus to 850. We have 750, minus 850. And now you could see we're doing basically our population variance formula over here, which each item minus the mean squared divided by the population. So now we're taking the subtraction point here and then we'll square it in the outer column. So we're going to take the 900 minus the 850, the 900 minus to 850, the 900 minus to 850. The one thousand minus the 850.

The one thousand minus the 850. And finally the one thousand. Minus the 850. Now we have these negative numbers and the positives. Now we're going to square them, which will make them all positive numbers and multiply and escalate the amount. So we're going to say this will be equal to two hundred fifty six carats and then two. So to the second power or the power of two or squared, I'm going to just copy that one down. And that should then have all the cells that would take the cell to the left and then to the power of two. So now we have squared them less than some of them up. So we'll go ahead and sum this up and let's go and underline Font and underline and some equals the sum of this data set. And that's going to give us 175.

Now, if we were then to take the population size, population size, that's in this formula. And so I'm going to do the count. It's ten because we have ten of them. But let's do the trustee count formula because that's the cool way to get it count. And that's just going to count that number of items in these cells. So I'm going to select these ten and they'll be ten of them. And then we're going to go to the front group and underline and then we want the state with the population variance, population variance being the one seventy five divided by the ten, that's going to give us the seventeen five for the population variance. But it's squared. So typically we want the standard deviation when we have our data set, which means we're going to take the square root. So equals the square root.

So I'm going to select that item and pick up the 75 square root of that would be the one 32 adding some decimals, no group, a couple of decimals there. And then we could take a look at the meaning. So we'll pick up the mean down here. And that's going to be equal to. And now what we calculate, Will, it's. This is the average Double-Click in the average selecting this data set. It's going to add them up and divide it by the number there, which would be ten. And there's the 850. We're going to then underline that font group and underline and then that's going to give us our coefficient coefficient of variation, which is going to be equal to the one thirty two point two nine divided by the 850. This number could be represented as a percent or decimal will keep it at the decimal.

At this point, it's about 16. Now, note, we'll get into more detail when we do some comparisons about how to analyze these numbers. Some of them, like the coefficient of a variation, will be more useful when we're comparing two different data sets. But just to get the standard process of calculating these, this is just how we might do it on a standard data set. And this is how you could kind of think of this scenario broken out into a standard data set where you normally do your kind of statistical calculations. You can also do that here, right? If we could put our answers in a little key with the Excel formulas or as many Excel formulas as possible, this would equal the average of these items.

And then we'd have the standard deviation, which could be the standard deviation. We're going to do the population size rather than the sample. So the standard deviation, dopy picking up this series of numbers again, that's going to then be the one 32, 29, then the variance. So this equals the variance once again, the variance of the population drop rather than the sample size. So we're going to go with the population for our purposes and select these again. And so there we have that. And then if we took just like the calculation down here, this would equal the standard deviation divided by the mean, and that would give us our percent, same percent over here if we add a couple more decimals on it.

So that's going to be one way we do it. Now, the way we'll typically see this then when we break this out, however, is not to break it out in a series of ten numbers, but I think that's a useful exercise to do. But we can then say, let's take our possibilities over here. We're going to pull in my same numbers, the 650. I'm going to copy that down. Let's do the autofill feature, copying that down to one thousand. Then we'll take a look at what is going to be the expected value. Expected value. I lost the expected here, let's say expected. We'll keep it just as expected, and then I'm going to say this is going to be equal, the one above it, and notice that basically the average of the mean.

Right. And so we'll copy that down. And then the difference is going to be the 650 minus to 850, the 750 minus to 850, the 900 minus the 850, and then the one thousand minus the 850. And now we're going to square it the way we normally do the way we kind of did over here. Right now, we've got our differences. Now we're going to square it. So let's say this is going to be equal to that number. I'm going to say shift six, which is the carrot to square it. Copy that down using the autofill autofill and copy that down. So there we have that and then we're going to basically add our probabilities at the end. So now we're going to add the probabilities as to we have that squared amount, which will be the twenty percent to twenty, twenty, thirty, thirty.

So twenty, twenty or thirty thirty. Let's take this whole four cells and make them a percent go into the No group percent to find them and I'll copy this down. So it picks up the twenty twenty thirty thirty, twenty, twenty thirty. And then we multiply this out forty thousand times the twenty percent and ten thousand times the twenty percent and this equals twenty five times the thirty percent. This equals the twenty, twenty five times the thirty percent. That's going to give us our six thousand seven fifty. Good. Then underline that font group and underline and our total. The total will then be equal to the sum of these items that'll give us our 75 and then we'll take the square root of that. So we'll take this square root and that'll give us well let's just call it the standard deviation. Let's call it the standard deviation which will be taken.

The square root equals square root. Selecting that item, square root of the 17 five notices, Of course, the 75 basically matches where we were here, that's like the population variance, right? So I have the total here we could label it might be better called the population variance, the 75 five. And then we take the square root and that's going to give us the expected value. So the expected value or we're going to pick up the expected value, which is the average which we calculated over here or we calculated there. And then I'm going to underline that font group and underline and the coefficient of variance.

Then the coefficient of variance is going to be equal to the 132 divided by the 850, adding a few decimals here. We then get to our same point one five, five, six. Now, a lot of times when we see problems like this, note that if you have one type of scenario you're going to do, oftentimes we're looking for that basically expected value and we might use that expected value as basically an estimate into the future. And then we might want basically to see the grouping around basically the average expected value and the population variance could give us an idea of that.

But if we have different kinds of options that we're looking at, then that's often when the coefficient of variation will come into play. So we'll do a couple more and just recalculate these a few more times and some practice problems in this format.

So we get comfortable with these numbers. And then we'll work more about comparing different projects, focusing more on the coefficient of variation and how that could be like a practical thing to be using when we're making different types of projections into the future.

Expected Value, Standard Deviation, & Coefficient of Variation

We have an advertising campaign that we're imagining to happen. This is one of many types of scenarios where you might go through this type of thought process. Then we're going to group our possibilities together and see if we can come into a systematic kind of grouping for them, add probabilities to them so that we can get a statistical type of analysis which could help us to move forward with a decision making process. So we're going to imagine then the outcomes, possibly based on looking at prior outcomes, are going to be grouped into either low average, high, very high. And then we're going to say that the outcome relative to that will be measured in units. So if the advertising campaign is low, possibly compared to prior advertising campaigns and projecting out into the future, we think we're going to get the seven hundred for that campaign.

If it's average, then we're thinking we're going to get 800 notice. Of course, these are kind of averages because if we look at prior campaigns, then we're looking at a range around their rights. We're probably picking, you know, the low ones on average, the average ones here, and then the high of the one thousand in a very high or good campaign, one thousand six hundred. So the next thing we would do is calculate or figure out what we think the probabilities will be of those results happening, the probabilities having to add up to 100 percent here. So we think that the low 30, average 30 high thirty and very high is

10 percent. So now we can look at that and try to figure out our expected value, which you could think about as kind of like the average value.

So we'll say this is going to be the 700 units for the low times, the 30 percent likelihood we'll take the 800 times, the 30 percent likelihood, the one thousand times the 30 percent likelihood and the 1600 times the 30 percent are the 10 percent likelihood. And that's going to give us our expected value. Now, we could think of that as kind of like the average value if we sum these up now equals the sum and that's going to be the nine 10. So we can basically think, OK, the nine, 10 looks about what we're going to say are kind of like the average or expected value based on the assumptions that were taken here. That's kind of like the average that we have now.

Oftentimes that's going to be a lot of calculations that you might do in many scenarios to come up with that number and use it going forward. We could go further than that and do more statistical analysis for it. Oftentimes when comparing multiple projects, we want to look at the variance of the variation, oftentimes looking at that coefficient of variation. So I want to calculate these and we want to look at them. And using our statistical tools are further statistical tools. And it could be a little confusing because if you've worked with data sets, then they don't lay out mostly this way. You're usually looking at a data set, which is like just a series of numbers and outcomes and whatnot. So let's put this into our series of numbers and outcomes.

Calculate it that way and then we'll do it the standard way for corporate finance with this kind of data set and see how the similarities look so we can apply our statistical kind of analysis and see what exactly we're doing with it. So let's just imagine if we had put in 10 numbers and 30 percent came out to be the seven hundred thirty eight hundred thirty one thousand ten at the one thousand six, let's just add those numbers in here and pretend that of 10 results, we got the 700. I'm going to make three of them because it's 30 percent, three of 10. Then we're going to take the 800, which is going to be once again, three of ten. Then we'll take the 1000, which will take three of those three of the thousand. And then finally, finally, the one thousand six hundred. I'm going to underline that. And so now we're mirroring this in ten results. We're imagining three at seven.

Three at the eight, three at the one thousand and 1600 at the ten percent at one thousand six hundred one of them. Something that up. We're going to call this the total sum. This equals m the S u. And so there we have that and then, then the next thing and notice we're basically doing this formula here, the population variance. So we're taken that each unit will have here minus the mean squared divided by the population. Size or the number of items, so we'll take the mean or the average. Now I'm going to put the meat all the way down. This is going to be equal to. I'm going to calculate it with the, um, I'm sorry, with the average function. Minar average average.

And then we'll just add these up or not add them or using the similar thing is the sum function, which is the series of numbers for those items we get the average of the nine ten, the average Of course, being the sum of these numbers divided by the the amount of items which are ten, which would be that nine thousand one hundred divided by ten or the nine ten. Now I'm going to say this equals the item above it. Put my cursor on that and copy that all the way down. Autofill that down will put an underlying. Well let's keep it there. We don't need an underline. We're not going to total up those and not let's subtract them out. So the value minus the mean.

So we're doing this calculation for each data point. We're going to say this, that 700 minus the nine ten the 700 minus the nine ten, the 800 minus the nine ten, the 800 minus the nine ten, the 800 minus the nine ten the 1000 minus the nine ten the 1000 minus the nine ten the one thousand minus the nine ten and the one thousand six hundred minus the nine ten. So now what we want to do is square them. That's going to be this part of the equation that'll make these negative numbers positive. So we're going to say this will equal this number, shift six to the carrot. In other words, two, squaring it, going to copy that down. It's going to autofill that on down autofill double click on the bottom one.

See if it looks like it should. It does. That's exactly what it should look like. And then we'll underline this item and let's go ahead and sum this up. Then we'll sum this up equals the S2 and the sum of these items. That's going to be six, six, nine thousand. And then we'll pick up the population size. That's just going to be the count. There'll be ten of them. I'm going to use the Excel function to count them. They'll equal the count shift nine and then select in this range of data. It'll just pick up the ones with items in it or ten of them underlining their font group and underline. And that's going to give us the population variance, population variance then being equal to the six, six, nine divided by ten.

That's basically this calculation in being in the population there. So now that still takes into consideration those squared items. So then we often want the standard deviation. Let's go ahead and pick it up from here, standard deviation. And for that, we'll take the square root to kind of get rid of the squared kind of component that equals the item above it. I'm sorry, not the item above. It equals the Q square root as Q Artie's the function for it, the 66 900. And so then let's add some decimals. No group, add in a couple of decimals, 258. Sixty five. And then we're going to pick up the mean or the average, the mean or the average which I could do it this way again.

Pick up the cell over here, I'll calculate it again with the average function that's going to be equal to the average average of this dataset that gives us the nine ten. Let's underline that front group and underline and then we have the coefficient of variation here and that's going to be equal to the 258 65 divided by the mean or average, we could percent to fight or simply add a few decimals, add a few decimals here. OK, so then we can do the same thing in our data set to the side. Oftentimes you'll see the data set over here if you just calculate this in Excel so we can calculate the average over here, which would be the mean. And so picking up the mean of these numbers, you can have the standard deviation, the standard s t I need an equal.

I was like, why didn't it wasn't anything showing up there, popping in there? And I'm going to take from the population rather than the sample. That's what we're going to be using, standard deviation of these items. So there's the standard deviation matching up. The variance would be equal to V, a R and we'll take it for the population again, variance for the population. Pick up these numbers and there is that. And then once again, once we have those, we can then take the standard deviation and divide it by the mean to get to the coefficient of variation that points to eight four to about add one more decimal there to match it up. OK, so that that's one way we can see it, that we might be more familiar with these calculations.

Oftentimes we'll be focusing here. If we're comparing multiple different scenarios, we'll see that in the future. But I just want to practice these calculations now. Let's do it the way we would do it normally. Here, if we didn't have the data set, we'll do kind of like the corporate finance kind of way where we're going to say right now, we'll pick up the same data, set the 700. And pull that down, I'm not going to break it out into like a series of 10, but I'm going to use the percentage of weights and you'll see how those come into play here. The expected value is going to be like the average, but we're going to have that's going to be like the expected value that we calculated. First here. You'll note that's the mean or average we calculated when we did our kind of data set over here.

And then we'll copy that down, copy that down the nine 10 and then we'll subtract them out, kind of mirroring this process. So now we'll subtract them out. This is going to be the 700 minus the 900. Let's copy that down autofill there. We have that and now we'll square it. Similar fashion as we did over here. So this is going to be equal, this item to the shift six or carrott to squaring it. Then we'll take that and copy it down, copying it down. So there we have it. And then we're going to apply our probabilities now. So now, once we squared it, this is the thing that's, you know, different from our data set here. We're going to take the probabilities which are going to be the thirty, thirty ten, thirty, thirty, thirty ten. And then let's select these three and go to the numbers. Make it eight percent.

Grab that thirty, drag it on down 30, 10, and then we're going to say this is going to be equal to the forty four, one times the thirty and let's autofill that and drag it down and that'll multiply them all across. So there we have that, let's total it up. Total is going to then be equal to the sum of these items and that's going to give us our 66 nine. Let's actually call that, you know, the population variance underline here font group and underline and then we'll take the square root, which we're going to call the standard deviation, the standard D equals. And that's going to be equal to the square root, square root of this number above it.

And to add a couple of decimals numbers, a couple of decimals. So that matches up here. And then we'll look at the expected values. So the expected value, let's pick that up over here, which we calculated the expected value is going to be equal to you. And that's basically the average, right? The average or the mean. A lot of different names for that one important number. We know what by many different names, it's been known by many names. And we're going to say this is the coefficient of variation which is going to be equal to the two fifty-eight divided by the expected value, mean average. And something went wrong. Hold on a second. This is divided by this. Add in a couple of decimals. Doo doo doo doo. There we have it. So there's the coefficient variance again.

And in practice, you might then be really looking for this if you're doing one kind of calculation, looking at your expected value of the nine, ten. And then again, if you're comparing different projects, oftentimes we're going to get down here to the coefficient of variance of variation, which could give us some idea about the spread of the data and give us some more indications about them, depending on the different data sets and what we're what we're trying to get from them. We'll do some comparisons in the future. But again, we just want to get used to the statistical kind of analysis and a couple of different scenarios on where you could apply that type of analysis.

Expected Value, Standard Deviation, & Coefficient of Variation

We're just going to say it could turn out bad, good or very good. So we have our three options here. Now, what would it mean to be bad? Well, based on prior information, we're going to say 600 on the unit sales. Good. We're going to say 800 and then very good, 1400. So we're going to assume we picked up this information based on prior sales or prior advertising we have put into place. Then we want to assign probabilities to them that will add up to 100 percent the likelihood that we believe each of these items will come to fruition. I'm going to sum these up. Obviously, the sum of them has to be equal to 100 percent. So we're going to say bad 30 percent, good rate 50 percent, and then very good 20 percent.

And so we're going to take these 600 times the 30 percent going to go ahead and copy that down for that being the autofill feature. So the 800 times 50 400, the 1400 times twenty is the 280 and underline here font group and underline and then sum it up with the equals CPM function adding those up. That's going to give us eight hundred and sixty. So we assume that to kind of be the expected value then which you can think of basically the average. That's what we're going to expect basically to happen given this set of scenarios and are weighted percentages. Oftentimes that is what we're looking for, but we might go further than that and try to think about, you know, other the variation of the outcomes that could be there, possibly looking for the amount of risk that might be involved.

This would be more applicable oftentimes when we're comparing two different data sets, which we'll do in future chapters. Note this time, unlike prior problems, we basically have the three categories here instead of the four categories you could have then multiple categories that might be involved in some kind of decision making process such as this. But your goal is basically group them together and put in those amounts that will be related to whatever it is that you expect to be happening for them and then weight them in such a way that they will add up to 100 percent so that you can calculate your expected value. So let's break this out into a series of numbers so that we can apply our statistical kind of calculations in the normal way.

And then once again, we'll do it in the way that basically we would expect to see within a corporate finance kind of calculation. So we'll see the similarities between the two. So let's imagine here that we have the 300. If we had the 600 at 30 percent, we would say that that would happen then. Six hundred three out of ten times. Let's just say we're going to have a series of ten numbers. We're going to say 600 will be three of them. 800 will be five out of the ten because it'll be 50 percent if we have ten numbers. So the 800, 800, 800, 800. That's five. Right, isn't it? One, two, three, four or five it is. I knew it. I knew I counted to five right there. And then the one thousand four hundred is going to happen two times. Two out of the ten being the twenty percent. Let's go ahead and total that up.

We'll have the total. This equals the sum of these items. And I'm going to underline that Ford Group and underline. And so there we have it now this would be a series of numbers that we could typically kind of do our statistical type of analysis with. But we can do something like that population variance now. So we're going to do that basically in an Excel worksheet. So to do that, we're going to calculate the mean or the average. So let's take the average of the series of numbers which we can calculate by saying equals average and then shift nine, taking this series of numbers right then and there and enter.

That's going to be our 860 notice that matches our expected value down here. And obviously, to calculate that with this series of numbers, we would add them all up and divide by then the amount of numbers, the amount of the population, which in this case is ten. So we're going to say this equals the eight sixty. Let's copy that down. Copy that on down. So every cell equals the one above it. Then we'll take the difference basically right here in the calculation. Now the numerator, we're going to take them the 600 minus the 860. The 600. Minus the 860. 600 miles to 860, the 800 minus the 860, the 800 minus the 860, the 800 minus 860, the 800 minus the 860, the 800 miners, the 860 and then finally the one thousand four hundred miners, the 860 and one four miners, the 860. So there we have it.

Now, let's go ahead and square these items. So we're going to square them now, basically doing this component of the equation. So we're going to say this is going to be equal to that number. Shift six, the carat to squaring it, pulling that on down, put it our cursor on it will handle dragging it on down. So there we have it going to underline font group and underline let's go ahead and sum it up now equals the Sum some function and some that up and then that's it. So now we can have a population size of the population size which measures just the number of items here, which were ten that's going to be at the bottom of our equation here. I'm going to do that with the cool count formula. So that's the best way to do the most impressive way to count these ones is just use the count function. And there it is.

It counted ten of them, just like we thought it would. And then we're going to go to the front group and underline and then we have the population variance, population variance say is equal to this one population variance is going to be equal to the eight zero four divided by the ten. Then we got eighty thousand four hundred. Now that's got those squared components in it. We're talking squared units at this point. What if they were dollar like squared? So we want the standard deviation typically. So let's pick up the standard deviation, which is the square root of that number equals the Q root security square root. In other words, of the eight thousand four hundred, add in a couple of decimals, thereby go into the number group testing the moralized and then we've got the stand.

That's the standard deviation. And then if we take the mean or the average to get to the coefficient of variation, let's calculate it again. It's that 868 or the 860 here or just the average average, which Of course is the mean average, same thing. So just keep that in mind. The median is different from the average. You recall all the stuff from statistical statistical Books, hopefully play some of it or it'll come back to you. It's all coming back now. I totally remember everything this time about statistics. So now we're going to say the eight to eighty three. Fifty five divided by the eight sixty and we'll then be going to add some decimals there. So there we have it. Now we're at the point three three zero point three three zero. So you could do that same kind of thing. You might see someone do this basically just in Excel. So if I wanted to just use Excel functions as much as possible.

And again, it's nice to see a series of numbers over here to actually do this calculation, because, again, this calculation here gives you an idea, pictorial idea about the data set. So it's kind of useful to actually do that. But if you just do this in Excel, obviously the mean of the median, we did that one. That's the average function average of this series of numbers right there, just as we saw before. There it is. We do the standard deviation equals the standard DSD, even with the top, because this is going to be for the population as opposed to the S for the sample size we're going to take we're going to assume total population formulas here. If you don't have one, you don't know what those two things mean.

Take a look at you know, there's a lot of statistical kinds, Of course, stuff on this that you can research on YouTube or whatever, wherever you want to go. So then the variance we got, the variance is going to be there and once again the population I'm going to pick up. So we'll pick up the population and then we have that. And then the coefficient is going to be the standard deviation divided by the average mean or median. And there we have that once again. If I add a couple more decimals here, we should come up to the same number and we do, just like we should have. OK, so now let's do the same thing. But now we're going to do it in kind of the corporate finance type of format. And so instead of breaking it out in the ten numbers and seeing a number set will apply our probabilities kind of at the end here.

So same kind of thing, though. We're going to pick up our possibilities. We only have three of them this time, which are going to be the 600. And then I'll copy that autofill two times down to sixty eight. And the one thousand for the expected value is the average value which we calculated over here at the eight sixty. The eight sixty. I'm going to say this equals the one above it and just bring that 860 all the way down. That difference is going to then be equal to the six hundred minus the eight sixty. Put our cursor on that and autofill it's down there. We have it now. We're going to square it. So similar kind of process over here, but we only have the three numbers because we're going to apply the probabilities next. And the next step, so this is going to be then that cell shift, six carrott to the power of two to the power of two squared.

In other words, I'm going to drag that down. So at two powers, the rest of them are squares, the other two, in other words, probabilities, then being the 30, 50, 20, 30, 50, 20. I'm going to select these three cells and make them a percent format, no group percent to fire them and then just simply copy that down and it should then pick up the relative cell references. And it did. It did what it should do. That's good. And then we'll just apply out the weights now at the end here. So that's sixty seven, six times the 30 percent, the three, six times the 50 percent and the two one six times the 20 percent. And then we have that put the underline over here font group and underline and then we have the total summing up. The total equals the S2 am shift nine of those three numbers. And so there we have it.

And that's going to be then instead of calling it total, I'm going to call it the variance. And then we want the square root, which is going to be the standard deviation. So now we'll calculate the standard deviation, which is going to be equal to the square root or the Scutari. That's how you do square root when you're doing it in Excel instead of that funny symbol over the top of the number. You know what I'm talking about? The little thing that goes over the top here, which is use the square root function. There we have it. And let's add some decimals, no decimals. And then we've got the expected value.

So the expected value type that and which is the average or mean expected value is going to be equal to the average or the expected value we got over here the A sixty underlining that put in a line underneath it, otherwise known as the underline. We're going to get the coefficient of variation, then coefficient of variation, the two eighty three point five five divided by the expected value and better then we have something funny happen. That's not right. That's not right. Hold on a second dividing and then add a couple of decimals. So there we have that, and so once again, this last number is often used when we do some more comparisons of different data sets and we'll take a look at some of those in the future. But just get a feel for this kind of statistical analysis of this and see how it kind of relates to a series of numbers, which might be where when you're thinking about these kinds of terms, you most likely would be applying them to a list of numbers.

Coefficient of Variation Three Investment Alternatives

We're not going to break it down into a list of numbers this time, but just use the standard calculation that's used for corporate finance generally with these types of calculations. So we'd have to figure out the investment. We're going to have investment one, two and three and then try to think about based on prior investment and, you know, different things with regards to the investment, what we believe the return will be possibly based on prior performance and similar investments and then judgments as to the economy going forward. And then we want to give our probabilities here to assign how likely we think that return would be and then we will calculate our expected value from it. So we're going to say if it's not a not a good return for option one, we're going to have 400 in terms of the return probability, going to be 20 percent if it does good. The possible average, we're going to say, is 800 based on prior performance.

We'll say that's going to be 20 percent likely and very good is actually higher, more highly likely, we're going to say is 60 percent likely that before we calculate that, just note in the second one here, we have different returns. For the second option, we're going to estimate different returns, but we have the same probabilities here of 2026. So same probabilities for option two. But with the 20/20 60 and then option three, we have different returns once again. And this time we have a difference in terms of the probability. So I got the 750 here. We got the difference in the probability. So let's do our calculations in a similar fashion as we did before. We're expecting this one 400, 20 percent likelihood.

So 400 times 20, then we'll take the 800 times the 20 percent likelihood and then the one 350 times the 60 percent likelihood. Obviously, the likelihood needs to be added up to 100. That then gives us our expected value, the expected value total in that 1050, which you could basically think of as kind of like the average value, what we expect to happen. So that's if you're thinking about a series of numbers, what we would think, it's kind of like the middle point or the average type of point, not the median, but the average, the middle type of point. And then we want to think about how much spread is going to be involved in that with regards to the data. And that spread then could be interpreted here as risk that would be involved.

So if we're saying that we think then the average return one thousand fifty and then we can think about how much risk there is involved with regards to the spread of the data based on this. So let's do that here. We're going to say then the return, let's say this is going to be equal to the 400. We're going to bring that on down for the three results here. So bring that on down with the autofill. The expected value, basically the average, the 1050, I'm going to just say this equals the one above it and the one above it. Then we'll subtract these two out. This being the four hundred minus to 1050, that's been the 800 minus to 1050. This being the one thousand three fifty minus the one thousand fifty, then we're going to square it as we did in the prior chapter.

So we're going to take then this number shift six or carat to the power power of two or squared and then we'll copy that on down, copying that on down. Then we got the probabilities that we're going to apply here that 2026 in this case, twenty. Let's make these three sales percentiles by going to the number of groups and make it a percentage sell twenty and then twenty and then sixty. Twenty, twenty, sixteen. That's what we got here. Then we'll take then this equals the four to five times the twenty percent. This equals 60 to five times to twenty percent. This equals the ninety thousand times the sixty percent underlying in here underlying that's going to be the total, the total sum in that up. This equals the sum of these items and enter.

We may also call that the variance and then we want the standard deviation. So we'll calculate through the standard deviation and that's basically that we square these items. So now we're going to basically square root it. Now, that would be the little symbol with a thing over the top of it. But in a. It would be equal to the square root formula or function of this item 151, so that's the square root. Let's add some decimals to it and we're going to the numbers group, add a couple of decimals, and then we want the expected value, which is kind of like the average. So that's going to be equal to what we calculated that one thousand fifty and then let's underline that font group and underline it.

And then we want the coefficient of variation, the coefficient of variation, which is probably what we should call this top term here, since that's what would be the bottom line that we're kind of getting to here. Let's do that and then let's divide this out.

This is going to be divided by that standard deviation, divided by the expected value. Add in some decimals. You could represent this in a percent or decimals put four decimals there. Now, this will make more sense, Of course, when we compare this to other ones so we can see what the average is that we expect to get from investment one, two and three clearly. And then the next thing we want to do is basically look at the risk, which is often going to be useful to look at the coefficient of variation in that case. All right.

So let's go to option two. I'm going to say this is going to be equal to this and this will be equal to this. Let's do it again y because it's good times. It's fun to do option two we got then this equals the seven hundred times to twenty percent. This is going to be the one thousand four hundred, ten times the twenty percent and then the two thousand fifty times the 60 percent. Obviously the percent should add up to one hundred and less. Something went horribly, horribly wrong or maybe not that horrible, but something would go wrong if that wasn't 100 percent. You would think that if we sum this up, that would be the expected value. So obviously, looking at these two, the expected value here is higher than the expected value there.

So it's like I like option two, then option two looks better. But then we want to think about, well, what's the risk that is going to be involved, you know, for us to, like, not be at that kind of center point or average, that's where the coefficient of variation comes into play. So then we're going to say, let's do this calculation. Then we got the seven hundred, then I'm going to copy that down for the three options here. We're going to say the expected value is the average then that we just calculated that one thousand fifty equals the one fifty one thousand six fifty, I should say, because that's the right thing to say and I'm trying to say the right thing instead of the wrong thing. And so then we're going to say the average or the expected value. Is that one thousand six fifty? So there we have it.

Wait, hold on a second. The difference is what we're looking for here. That's what it says in the column titled The Difference is going to be the 700 Mindszenty one six five oh, the one thousand four hundred miles, the one six five oh oh oh, the 20 50 minus the one six five oh oh oh. And then we're going to square it by taking that cell shift, six carrott to two, squaring it to the power of to the to power, to power square power. So there we have that and then we'll take the probabilities. In 2026 I'm going to select these three cells first, make them percent format by going into the no group percent format and then we'll pick up the 20 and then just simply autofill it.

Let's do it with a copy and pasting this top, copy it down, arrow shift down control the pasted that sixty's obviously coming from there it looks good. Then we'll multiply this out. We've got nine to five times the twenty. Let's do our copy and paste here. Control see down arrow shift holding down down arrow control the pasted. It has been pasted and pasted has been done. And then we're going to go to the font group and underline this is going to be the very end variance. So the variance is going to be equal to the s u m shift nine up arrow hold and shift up up and enter. Then we want the standard deviation because that's like a squared number and we want to take the square root of it equals the square root of it. Square root.

It is going to give us that number of the 538 numbers group adding a couple decimals to that. And then if I want to compare them to this data set up here, which had different numbers in it. Right. This took this function of standard deviation, took away that squared component. So now we're talking about actual dollar like units. But again, it's not as easy to compare like the spread or the variation from the deviation. And you'll note that these two basically have similar kinds of probabilities here. So that's when the coefficient of variation comes into play. And we're going to bring it into play right now. It's going to be brought right into play right here.

So we want the mean then the expected value, average or mean, and then underline that font group and underline and now finally what we've been waiting for, the coefficient of variation being equal to this, divided by this and adding some decimals, no group adding some decimals. So there we have it. So three to five eight here versus the three seven oh one. So we have the notice. We had the same weightings here, but obviously on different different dollar amounts. So we have a different basically coefficient of variation. Now, if you want to analyze that a little bit more, just to see how that works out in a number series, you can do what we did in prior chapters and break these both out into basically ten numbers.

You know, where you have the four hundred four hundred hundred, eight hundred and six of these and then do your same kind of calculations and you might get a better understanding of what's happened or picture this data set a little bit differently. OK, let's do it one more time for the last one. This one, we have different probabilities here. So let's do this one. This is going to be equal to 750 times the forty percent. I'm going to copy it down this time. Control see down arrow shift control. Summing this up. This should obviously add up to that 100 percent. Again, the expected value summing this up gives us the two thousand one thirty. Now, the 2001 thirty is obviously higher than the other two.

So everything else being equal, we would then, Of course, like that one. But then we want to think about, you know, what's the risk for that potential return that we might get. Right. So we're going to see the risk, we're going to say the return. If we get the seven fifty, copy that down, control C down, shift down, control V and then we'll take the expected value, which is kind of like the average that we just calculated right there equals the one above it and the one above it. The difference is the subtraction, the seven fifty minus the two three two one three zero, the twenty five five zero minus two one three zero, the one thousand fifty minus two one three zero. There we have that now we're going to square them equals this item.

Shift six carats to the power of two otherwise known as squaring it, copying that, pasting it on down control v and then we squared all these two. Same thing because these are hard coded numbers and they copied down with us and then the probabilities. Forty 420. Let's select these three cells and make them the percent type cell number of the group percent type cell and then we'll take. We'll take the percent 40 and then copy that one down control, see down shift down arrow control V and then it picks up the relative cell references and now will multiply it across. This equals this squared Eitam times to 40 percent copy and that down control see down arrow shift down control v make an underlying font group and underline.

And then this is going to be the variance, the variance being equal to the sum of shift nine up arrow holding shift these three cells. Then we want to take this standard D, the standard D and that's going to be equal to the standard deviation. Hold on a second. Square root equals the square root. Square root. That's how you do the standard. There is a standard formula, but we're taking the square root here. So in any case, we're going to take the expected value now so that we can get down to the coefficient of variation. So the standard value is going or the expected value we calculated to be that two thousand 130 underlining that fine group and underline we then get the coefficient of variation, the coefficient of variation.

Is this divided by that standard deviation, divided by the expected value? No group adding some decimals. So there we have it. Now, once again, if you look at this as just the first calculation, you're going to say, well, this one, the expected value, what we expect to happen from these three investments, the higher the number, the better. Right. But then when you're looking at the coefficient, the larger this number, then the more risky it is. So when you're looking at the risk, you would say this one would be the least risky, right? That would be the least risky. And then this one would be second on the risk.

So you want lower numbers here on the risk assessment and then the most risky one would be down here. And that's kind of like what you would expect, obviously, because with the higher amounts here or the higher possible gains you would expect the higher risk possibly to be aligned with that. So those are the two things that you're always trying to measure when you're projecting out into the future, the possible gains that might be there and then the risk that's associated with those gains that you want to take into place. So for a book problem, then you'd be saying or in practice, but the book problem will often be emphasizing the coefficient of variation to think about the risk. And they might ask something like, you know, if you are a risk averse person, which one would you pick? And you'd pick, you know, the least risky one, which would be possibly this one.

And notice, this one has a higher expected return and it's less risky than the second option. Right. So the first option is, you know, even if you're more, you probably wouldn't be picking it because it's basically got, you know, a lower return than the second option. And it's got more risk than the second option. Right. And then so you'd probably be saying this would be the least the one you'd pick if you're risk averse. And if you don't mind risk and you're willing to take on a risk in order to get a higher return, then you might be more inclined to pick the third one here. You know, that would be the standard kind of process from basically the coefficient of variation or the standard kind of set of questions you might get with relation to the results on it.

Coefficient of Variation & Investment Risk

If you want to think about that calculation, take a look at some prior chapters, as well as the standard deviation, which helps us to kind of think about the spread from the mean. Again, to get more concepts on that, take a look at some prior chapters where we calculate that now, although the standard deviation gives us some idea about the spread from the mean, it's not something that we can typically be comparing to different investments that have different returns on it. So what we want to do is calculate the coefficient of variation. So let's think about that, that that's going to be calculated as the standard deviation divided by the expected return. And we have the decimals in place here. So they've got the three decimals.

If you need decimals, you go to the numbers group, add some decimals here. It's going to be rounded about the point, seven, six, five. Now, that number makes more sense when we compare it to other kinds of options that we have. So if we go on through here to the same thing, standard deviation divided by the expected return, this will be the standard deviation divided by the expected return. This will be the standard deviation divided by the expected return and finally, the standard deviation divided by the expected return. Now, looking at these on the expected return itself, then, Of course, if we were just to see these in total, the higher the better, right. We would say, OK, five looks good. And then these two are basically the same and then one here.

But then we also want to think about what's going to be the risk that's going to be away. Meaning if these are the mean or the average, how likely is it that we're going to be away from the average? And how can we compare that likeliness to other investments, even if they're not basically of the same size? So we can then that's where the coefficient of variation goes. And so which is going to be the one that is least risky here, least to greatest risk, this one with the lowest coefficient would typically be the least because it has the least variation from the center point. And then we're going to say this one, the next one up is going to be two. And then we have this one that is going to be the next one up on three. And then we have four here and five up top, five up top. So there we have it. So then again, that would be another concept that you'd want to take into place.

So if you were very risk averse, then the one here is the first option that you would have, even though you have to compare the expected return and the level of risk. And then number two, you have the next level up here. This is at thirty one thousand and one is at thirty one thousand two. So between these two, you would think that you'd want to be picking basically one, since you have the same kind of expected or average return and you have less risk involved in it, less movement away from that from that center point. So you would think between these two, you might choose that the first one and then if and the third one out in terms of risk is going to be here. So notice as we go up in terms of risk, you would think that if you're going to take on more risk, it would be in order to get a higher expected return. Right.

If I'm going to take on more risk. The only reason I would want to take on more risk or I might want to take on more risk is because the expected return for doing so would then be higher. And then notice that this one, you've got an expected return of 50, this one an expected return of one seventy six, which is quite a bit higher, and this one up five. That which is the highest ranking for the coefficient variation has the most risk involved in it. So that one doesn't look like a very good option at all, considering the fact that you could get one with an expected return possibly down here that would be higher and have a, you know, a lower risk amount at even this one with the higher or the highest expected return with the lower risk.

So you could see it kind of what you would normally expect is the level of risk goes up and possibly the level of return goes up and adds the level of risk goes up. We might be more willing then, Of course, to take to take. I mean, as the level of expected return goes on, we might be able to take on or might. Want to take on more risk if the expected return goes up and the risk goes up, it goes down, or if the expected return goes down and the risk goes up, then then, Of course, we would want to basically not take on more risk if we don't get a better return results possibly from it. So that would be the general idea. And you can kind of see that happening here.

We got the first one and the third one again, the second one. Notice it didn't go up here, even though the risk went up. So, again, I might not choose one of these two. And then number three, as the risk went up, the expected return went up. And then we got the expected return goes up quite a bit as the risk goes up, too. And then again, one here up top is kind of the outlier, doesn't really fit in the system. It is probably one we wouldn't be considering, given the fact, again, the expected return is much lower and we can think we can pick basically, you know, any of any of these items down below and have a better expected return at a lower level of risk.

Expected Value & Net Present Value Even Yearly cash Flows

We're going to imagine a situation with a capital budgeting type situation where we have that initial investment of fifteen thousand five hundred, the life is going to be five years. We're imagining in this situation, then we're going to have even inflows from this investment. We don't know what those inflows are, but we're going to imagine for the next five years, four, five years out, that this piece of equipment will have even inflows as we go through the next five years. So then we're going to apply our statistical kind of thought process to this. Now, in the past, we've done these capital budgeting types of decisions matching different kinds of decision options, making assumptions about what is going to happen in terms of cash flow into the future. Obviously, those are assumptions.

So this will help us. This framework can kind of help us to make possibly some of those assumptions that we can then use to be compared with other types of capital projects. All this stuff, Of course, is happening into the future. We don't really know what's going on. We can just basically group our thought process in the best way we can to make as logical a decision or prediction into the future that we can. So note, if you're looking at a situation like this, there's basically two ways that we can use our analysis down here. We got these different categories that we're going to work these into and our probabilities to help us group the information in our mind. If we were to think of this capital budgeting type of situation as having even cash inflows, these options, then whether they be good, not good.

So on representing even cash flows for the next five years, this would be in the annual cash flow, then we can basically use that and do our probability calculation and then the result, the expected value, the expected annual return, then we can use and calculate our net present value using that amount. However, if we have a situation the other way we could do this is we could basically calculate the net present value for each of these imagining these happening, you know, net present value in each of them five years out and then taking the net present value calculations and applying basically our probability kind of calculation based on that which we might do in a future chapter.

Now, note that the first method that we'll do now we can only do if we assume even cash flows into the future, if there were uneven cash flows into the future, then we couldn't do this method. We would then have to do the present value of the cash flows and then and then apply this kind of thought process on the net present value, which we might do in a future chapter. So we're going to assume here that we have the possibilities and you don't really need the possibilities over here. But I'm just going to list them in words just so we can have some categories. So not good. OK, good. Very good. The numbers, Of course, are what's going to be important.

Where would we get these numbers based on prior performance, possibly other equipment, possibly other companies doing similar types of things, trying to estimate what their possible returns are from it and then projections out into the future? Again, we don't know exactly. Our goal is to put this into a framework where we can get our mind working in such a way that we can make some predictions, hopefully, as logically as possible. So we're going to say four thousand five hundred six thousand eight thousand five hundred ten thousand. Those are the inflows per year for the next five years that we are assuming. So then we want to say, let's assign some probabilities and then get to our expected inflow for the next five years based on that. So we're going to say the first one.

Twenty percent likelihood, then the second one. Thirty percent. Third one thirty percent. Fourth one is the twenty percent. If we sum that up then we get to one hundred percent. Of course then we can calculate our expected value, which would be the four thousand five hundred times to twenty percent. The six thousand times the thirty percent, the eight thousand five hundred times to thirty percent. Ten thousand times twenty percent. Summing that up with the equals S2 and shift nine and sum it on up front group and then underline. So there's going to be what we assume to be our cash flow. So now we're again assuming that to be our yearly cash flow for the life of this equipment of the five years, then we can use the.

To do our net present value calculation and possibly use that to then compare against other projects so we can then say, let's do our calculation of top zero, one, two, three, four or five years. I'm going to center those items by going to the alignment and center cash flows. We're going to say outflow negative one thousand five or 15 five. And then it's going to be equal to our expected value of 7000 to fifty, which is our annual cash flow.

So we'll bring that on down. You might say, hey, look, that's an annuity. Why don't we use the annuity calculation? I'll do that later. We'll do it with the annuity, too. So let's drag this on down. And this is going to be the total.

Now, the fact that these are even that's what I'm talking about with regards to these being even if these were not even cash flows, these these options not representing even cash flows, then we might have to do this net present value first for each of the options and then maybe we can use those in results to do it through a framework like this, which we might look at in a future chapter. All right. Let's do our present value calculation, negative present value shift nine. I'm going to go through this fairly quickly because we've done a lot of these in prior chapters. If you want more detail on them, I go back to those prior chapters. So I'm going to pick up the rate, which is going to be our cost of capital down here. And I'm going to make that an absolute reference.

F4 on the keyboard dollar side before the B and the 13 comma number of periods is zero, which means we're going to get to the same result here, but then I'll be able to copy it down, comma, comma, because it's not an annuity, but present value of one will do it in an annuity shortly and that's going to be the 15 five. We come to the same number because we're a period zero. But let's copy that down. Putting our cursor on the fill handle and dragging feel handled down. Then if I double click on one down here, it does look like it's doing what it's supposed to do. So that's a good and fine group and underline and let's sum it up, summing it up.

So then we get the nine thousand three ninety, which we can then say, well, that cleared zero, that's above zero. So it cleared the rate of fourteen percent. So you can see how we can imagine this to happen because again, we don't know what these numbers are. We could do this outcome and we could net present value each one of these for outcomes, like we say, and then try to do some kind of statistical analysis. But the bottom line is we got to get to some number here that we can then compare possibly to other projects. So this is one format that we can frame our thought process in order to do that. We can see here that based on this analysis, we've cleared the 14 percent. What rate are we at? What if we wanted to compare this to other returns or other projects or other equipment that is clearing the hurdle rate of the fourteen percent? We can calculate the IRR, which is equal to the error IRR or shift nine, and then I just pick up this flow.

And we then get to the thirty seven point one three, that's pretty good, it seems like that's the rate at which this net present value based on these cash flows would be zero. And then just note that we could calculate this with an annuity calculation, which I kind of like this calculation. If you have Excel, annuity calculations are often what's going to be done in book problems because they're trying to lower the amount of calculations if they take away your calculator and whatnot. But in practice, it's kind of nice to have, you know, each of the yearly flows to excel really has a better rechapter, I think, in that format. But test questions have a different objective right there trying to test you on stuff.

So if you're calculating or getting ready for a test, they might limit you for other reasons. So the annuity, then let's do the annuity type of calculation. This would be the negative present value shifts nine. The rate would be 14 percent. And again, we have chapters on how to do the annuity with a formula and how to do it with tables if they make use of tables in prior chapters. You can take a look at those there. I won't go into a lot of detail here with that number of periods. We're going to say five and this time it's an annuity. So we're just going to say the annuity or is the payment, which is going to be that seven thousand to fifty seven thousand to fifty. And then we have the initial investment. So the investment, which was equal to, I'm going to say negative of the 15 five.

And that's going to give us the total now, which is going to be equal to the sum, as you are, of the nine. Let's do that again equals LSU. And shouldn't it be positive I must put in that. Yeah. So there it is. So that's how we can calculate it that way too. So any time you see a series of payments that are the same, you might think of annuity, but just realize that Of course you can do either one. It's not like, you know, these two things are related, Of course. So but again, in a test question, it is more likely if they make all the payments the same and take away your calculator and give you tables or something to do an annuity calculation. But you can see how the same method here basically can be applied to different things when we're trying to structure our thought process in the future and we don't know what's going to happen. Right.

And we're trying to put the stuff together in such a way that we can come up with a prediction. And here's our prediction. And you can imagine a situation where there's large capital projects and you're competing with other people that all have their own personal interests on the capital projects. And, you know, you know the numbers. You know, you're trying to come up with numbers that are predictive into the future here. And that's all, it's all predictions that are taking place, Of course. But you're trying to make them as accurate as possible so that you can kind of compare these things out. Right.

So we got our prediction on the annual values that we got to do the present value. And if we're competing with other kinds of projects or there's other projects we're deciding on, then we might take the internal rate of return if we can only pick some projects and not the others. And again, you could see how all of this is an attempt to be, you know, as scientific as possible about an approach, even though we don't know, because we're looking out into the future.

Expected Value & Coefficient of Variation Investment Options

Obviously, when we're thinking about investments, we're usually measuring between the possible return that could take place and the level of risk that that will be involved. And clearly then we might want more risk. We might be willing to accept more risk if there's going to be a higher expected value. If there's more risk and the expected value is lower, then obviously that's an easy type of decision to make. Right? If the expected value is higher and there's more risk, then the question is it could depend on how much risk you're willing to take in and how much risk you want in your current portfolio compared to everything else and that type of analysis.

So we're going to have our same kind of thought process. I'm going to put the categories you don't really need the categories on the left hand side, but the idea is that you're going to try to make some type of projections out into the future and then use our statistical kind of analysis to basically get the expected value. And then we'll take a look at the coefficient of variation, possibly to compare it to other investments that do not have the same kind of returns structure. And that'll allow us to give us an idea of the disbursement and give us an idea of the volatility kind of activity around, you know, the means to give us an idea about the risk that would be involved.

So we would have to group these. How would we know about the grouping of them? We can look at the prior returns that have been received in the past, possibly, and then make projections into the future. And so in this case, we're going to group from the not good. OK, good. Very good. Extremely good. You don't really need the words in the category, but we need to categorize them in some way. And that's going to be in numbers here. The 600, the 650, the 800, the 950 and the one thousand notice investment two. We only used the four categories. So the number of investments, the number of categories isn't particularly important. Obviously, what you need to do is make sure whatever categories you have that you can weigh them.

And weighting in those categories is something that you're going to have to once again use past performance and then projections about into the future. The sum of the weights should be one hundred percent. So adding those up gets us to that 100 percent. So then if we multiply this out, we're going to take the 600 times the twenty percent that's going to give us the 120 to 650 times the twenty percent. It's going to give us 130 800 times the twenty percent. It's going to give us 160. The 950 times the twenty percent. The one ninety and the one thousand times the twenty percent gives us the two hundred.

Summing that up equals the stem cell. I mean it is going to give us 800 dollars. That's going to be our expected value then. So if we compare that to the second one down here, we're going to do the same thing. We're going to imagine this is investment two. We have a different set of numbers here that will be used in different probabilities. And let's get our expected value there. We'd say the 650 times the 40 percent, the 700 times the 20 percent, the 800 times the 10 percent and the 900 times the 30 percent. Obviously, the percent once again adding up to 100 percent. And the expected value equals the sum of these items. And that's going to be the 750.

So in this case, the 750 clearly is lower than the 800. So all else equal, we would want to be choosing the one that has the higher expected value. But the other thing we need to take into consideration is the level of risk that would be involved and we could use that's where the coefficient of variation often will come into play here. So let's calculate that we could say this is going to be our six hundred, so we'll pick up the 600. I'm going to copy that down just to get our series. So I'm just going to control it. There's a series of numbers. Then we're going to get the expected value, which you could think of as kind of like the average or the mean, the expected value that we have just calculated average or mean being the more statistical type of terms when we use this kind of analysis and just a series of numbers situation going to copy that on down. So there's the 800 all the way down. We're going to take the difference.

Then I'm going to take the six hundred minus the 800 negative two hundred the 650. Minus the 800. The negative 150. The 800 minus. 800 the zero, the 950 minus the 800 is going to be 150 to 1000, minus the 800 is 200, then we're going to square it. So this is going to be equal to the 200 shift, six with the carrot, two for the square going to copy that control. See go on down shift and down control the. So we have now squared all of them. They have now been squared, they're all a bunch of squares now and then we're going to take the probabilities which were 20, 20, 20, 20, 20. So the 20 percent. Let's go ahead. And percentiles, this whole column selected in this column and the numbers percentiles, they have been percentages and then I'll copy that.

Down control, see down arrow holding shift down, down, down to control V and then we'll take our our multiplication forty thousand times the twenty percent going to copy that down control see down arrow holding down shift down down down control the underlining on down below font group and underline summing it up with the equals. Assume the trustees some function. Our favorite of all the functions. That's everybody's favorite function. If it's not your favorite function then you're wrong. Your favorite and this is wrong. In this case there is a correct answer to favorite functions in Excel and it's the sum function. And so then we're going to say that this is going to be squared so this has then our R squared items in it. So now we're going to take the standard deviation. So this notice, this number would be like in square dollars.

So that's why the standard deviation is to bring us back in the units that we're in. So we're going to say this is going to be the square root, which is that little, you know, the thing that goes in over the top. But in Excel, it equals the square root as the formula of that number takes the square root of it. Let's add a couple pennies here. So we go to the number of group, add a couple of decimals to see the sense since has been made because since has been added we have added since to the calculation and then we're going to take the expected value, which is the kind of like the average is basically the average or the or the mean to get to our coefficient of variation. Bottom line, the line on the bottom equals the one fifty eight eleven divided by the eight hundred. And so hold on a second.

That's not right. The one fifty eleven divided, divided by there we go and then we can add some decimals. You might see it as a percent, you might see it as decimals. We'll bring it out to four decimals here. So this number doesn't make much sense in and of itself. If we were to look at this calculation by itself, we might then focus just simply on the expected value and possibly the standard deviation. But when we do the comparison down below, then that's when this number could give us a relative comparative value. So let's go down here. We're going to say, let's pick up these same numbers, the six fifty, and we'll copy that on down control. See holding shift down down control the pasting it out, the expected value then being equal to the seven fifty. This equals the seven fifty copies.

In that case turning it on down below will take the difference which is going to be the six fifty minus the seven fifty. This is negative one hundred the seven fifty minus the 700 minus to 750 negative fifty. The eight hundred minus to seven fifty fifty. The nine hundred minus the seven fifty. The one fifty. We're going to square them now take the square, let's square all these ones. This equals that number. Shift six carats to the to power power of two which is what you do when you square it. Copy and control see down arrow shift down down. Control the pace, turn it on down. We have now squared them all. They are all squares now. Now we'll take the probabilities which are going to be equal to forty percent over here. I'm going to select these cells and make them percent type cells by going into the no group and percentages in them.

Then let's copy that control. See down, shift down down and control the pasting them on down and then we'll go ahead and multiply this out ten thousand times to forty percent. Copy that control. See down down down. Control V there we have it then underlined font group and underline and then we'll sum it up for the eleven for the eleven thousand five hundred eleven thousand five hundred. Let's put an underlying there. We've done that already. Let's go ahead and label that that's going to be equal to or pick up the same labeling standardization, the very the variance we want then the standard deviation so that we could bring it back into non square dollars by taking the square root, which in Excel is the q r t formula. Shift nine. There it is.

Square root is. 107 adding some pennies, let's put some sense to this, let's make some sense out of this cell and then we'll take the expected value, which is kind of like the average of the mean. And that's going to be equal to what we calculated over here, the 750, 750, we might have some pennies there. We have pennies now. We don't need pennies on it. We don't need cents since it is not necessary for that. So that still can make no sense. And then the coefficient of variation, this is going to be equal to the 174 divided by the 750, adding some decimals. No group. Let's put it back to the four there. And so we have the four decimals. They're now comparing these to this one being the higher coefficient of variation has more variance from the mean would be the more risky.

So this one would be the one that has more risk that would be involved, and that's kind of what we would expect. So then that makes the decision a little less clear. So, I mean, if you're a risk averse person, then you might choose this one, even though the expected value is lower. If you're willing to take on the risk, you might choose this one, even though the risk is higher because the potential return is higher. Note that if you came up with a situation where the coefficient of variation resulted in this one being more risky than this one, then you would think, I'm sorry if it came up with this one being more risky than this one. The reverse situation, meaning the expected return, was both smaller and had a higher risk.

That's when the decision would be very straightforward. We would say, oh, well, you know, I mean, if we did this right, you would think that this investment up here would be the way to go because it has less risk. And it would be if that were the case. It's not the case here. But if that were the case, if you had an investment that had less risk and a higher return, that would be a straightforward decision, assuming all your thought process was correct if you had. But this would be the more normal and confusing situation, which is often the case, because the higher returns typically come coupled with a more risky item in it. So the question is, how much risk are we willing to take on with relation to the higher potential rewards? And that leads people to believe. Note that every time you take on more risk, there's a higher reward.

There's not a higher I mean, it could be it could quite well be the situation that one investment has a higher risk and a lower reward, which means it's pretty easy in that case. You want to weed that one out. It is not good as not a good one. But if there's a higher reward and there's higher risk to it, then the risk that you're taking on might be worth it, given the fact that for that higher reward, especially if it's in alignment with some other kind of asset groups possibly that you have in a portfolio as well, if that's what you're looking for in terms of of of your your spread of investments and whatnot.

Expected Value in Capital Budgeting Decision Uneven Payments

We want to do our present value analysis with a net present value calculation and the internal rate of return. Generally, the two main tools to help us to determine whether or not it would be worthwhile for us to put money into that particular project and or compare that project to other projects. Now, when we do this when we do this type of analysis, obviously everything that we're putting into it is a projection when we think about the future cash flows and whether or not it would be worthwhile to put money in it, well, then we have to come up with those future cash flows, which again, are in the future, we don't really know. So we might apply our analysis in this format to try to group the thought process there, to figure out what the future cash flows would be.

And we might say, OK, I want to say, well, this is what it would look like if it was a very good outcome. OK, not good. We don't need this kind of terminology, by the way, but that might help us to kind of categorize between three to five categories typically, and then do our probability type of analysis. Now, in a prior chapter, we had a situation where we assumed that we had even cash flows. That would be the result. In other words, if you're putting the one hundred thirty thousand down and you assume even cash flows are going to result for the next five years, then you could basically do this analysis on an annual cash flow type of basis so that we can get then our expected value on which we can then calculate the net present value calculation.

However, if we have uneven cash flows, meaning the annual cash flows, we don't really know. We might not even know, you know, exactly how long the inflows will be or something like that. So we might then have more nuanced, basically projections about what might happen. It might last, you know, might we might have inflows for the next five years. We might have inflows for the next ten years, and we might have different kinds of probabilities in terms of how long the project will last and in the inflows might be different. It might not be an annual inflow that will be the same. It might go down each year. We might say we'll get a bigger and bigger cash back at the beginning than later.

Well, then we can't really use this kind of analysis with the annual cash flows that we would then present value. But we might still be able to use this kind of analysis by running those different scenarios. So in this case, with investment one and investment two, we might think of different scenarios that we might have, and those scenarios could have varied cash flows and they could have varied years that the cash flow might be coming in. We could then present value each of those different scenarios using our net present value techniques, which you can then take a look at in prior chapters where we've taken what we've gone over, that once we have the net present value of the inflows, after we have net present value them, then then we might be able to apply an analysis such as this and do our similar kind of analysis. So we're imagining this particular investment, which would have a one hundred and thirty thousand hour outflow up front.

We come up with three different scenarios as to what might happen with regards to that, to the outcome of that one hundred and thirty thousand. We're going to assign probabilities to them and then we're going to present the value of each one of them. So if we present the value of each of the inflows that are going to result based on our three different scenarios for this one investment, then we can compare that to the initial investment here, which is going to be the one hundred thirty thousand outflow. So we're imagining we present value just the inflows. Now we're comparing that to the outflow. If we sum that up, then we'd have the net present value that we would then calculate here.

Now note again, when we do the net present value, the discount rate would kind of be included in that. So we're trying to basically compare these items after the net present value calculation and then we can try to do our probability type of analysis at the 2060 twenty scenario one being twenty percent, likely sixty percent for scenario two and then scenario three at the twenty percent. This would then add up to one hundred percent. And we can do our calculation here, which would be sixty thousand times twenty percent. We've got the 70000 times the 60 percent and the 40000 times the 20 percent, something that we would then have the expected net present value of 46000.

So, again, this is a little reverse of a problem we had in the past where we did the net present value of the annual payments, which we then took that expected value and did the net present value calculation. In this case, we did the net present value calculation first because of possibly uneven payments, and then we got to the expected net present value in our probabilities. If we did that down here on the second one, then we might do the same thing. We have three different scenarios. We ran the net present value for the three different scenarios with different payments possibly over the years, and the life could be different for them and whatnot.

And then we're going to say that the cost, the outflow up front for the capital budget is 200000. The difference then is going to be equal to the 400 minus 200 I'm sorry, plus because it's a negative to negative number, but we'll subtract them out, will copy that control, see pasting it on down and then apply out the net present value, the 200 times the 50 percent, the one 10 times the 20 percent and then the 150 times the 30 percent. And we could sum these up equals the sum. And that would give us our expected value, expected net present value. Now, in this type of calculation, when we're comparing these two, this would give us some indication of this one obviously being higher on the net present value.

We do have some of our STEM limitations with the net present value calculation just in general, because we have in this case, different investment amounts, which could have an impact on the net present value. But in general you have the net present value. The higher it is, the better. So generally you would think that this would be an analysis for Project two, but you might do further analysis with the internal rate of return and so on and so forth with regards to these. But this is, again, another approach that we could use for the capital budgeting decision, where you can use this kind of framework for different scenarios that might be taking place in the future, which can better help group your idea. So notice it again. This probability assumption could be used in many different many different scenarios. We're trying to think into the future. And you're trying to group your ideas together to predict or predict what might happen in the future.

What Next

How much are we going to get back in the future? Now, we could use our statistical type of analysis to try to think about each year that's going to happen into the future. So, for example, we might say we're going to have that initial investment going out. We're going to say the 1400 cost of capital discount rate is going to be 15 percent. And then we might say, well, in year one, let's predict how much we're going to get back and possibly use our scenario here to do so, say if it was low average or high on a year by year basis. So let's imagine in year one we're going to say, well, if it was low, we're going to imagine we get the 300 back. If it was averaged four hundred and high at one thousand and then try to wait that out.

So that's another way that we could basically try to break down a capital budgeting project on a year to year type of basis to think what the cash flows would be as the cash flows come in on a year to year type of basis. And then we'll have to apply our percentages. This being 40, 20, 40, we're going to make it a little bit more confusing as well. Just to show some variation here. Note that we could then say, well, if the capital project had a year or two revenues do the same thing for a year to add year three. We're going to imagine here that we're only getting revenue back periodically for this type of capital project that's going into play here. So the next year that we're going to get back, we're saying is year three. So we had revenue coming back in year one, no revenue in year two.

And then we're going to have the disbursed revenue in year three, where we're going to apply the same type of analysis. So in year three, we're going to imagine low average or high returns that on these numbers, the non discounted numbers, we're going to average or assume what we're going to get here. And then we'll apply our percentages for this year of the receipt and then we'll do the same for the next year. We're going to imagine we're not going to get any more money until year nine. So then year nine, we've got cash flows from the same initial investment. And we're going to apply our analysis of the four hundred, the eight and the nine and the rates at the forty 40.

So then once we do that, we can then try to use our present value type of analysis here to then present value our expected returns, the expected returns, not for the full project now, but on a year by year type of basis. So let's see what this would look like. So we're going to say this is going to be for the first year, we're putting 1400 down for the first year. We're going to assume these three options that we might get. And we have the rates at the forty, 20, 40. So we're going to say 300 times the 40 percent. We've got 800 times the 20 percent and then 1000 times the 40 percent. Adding those up, summing up, we get the expected value.

Obviously the total percentages have to add up to one hundred percent. Note that the names low average high are not really necessary here, but they might help you to just get an idea of what the numbers are meeting. Obviously low on the cash flow inflow. The lower number is not as good and then higher as good, good or better and so on. And then we'll do the same for the second one. So the second one, this is year three. So we're imagining dispersed inflows from the same capital budget outflow. It could be year to year. You could do the same thing on a year by year basis. Imagining the cash flows would be different from each year. And try to do that, figure that out. But we're going to say this is going to be 500 times the thirty percent.

This is going to be 800 times the forty percent. This is going to be the 1002 times the thirty percent summing up the percent. They, Of course, need to add up to one hundred, summing up the amounts for the expected value. Then they add up to an expected value of eight thirty for this year. And then we have year nine, same kind of scenario. We got these three estimates that we're going to make and then the percentages that we're going to be thinking happens out in year nine. So four hundred times the 40 percent, 800 times the 20 percent, 900 times the 40 percent underlying in that Ford group underline let's sum these up equals the S you are and picking those up and summing up for the expected value, this time being the six hundred and eighty.

So now that we have these. Affected values from the inflows, then we can present value. So we've now looked at the future inflows on a yearly basis, then we can apply our net present value to those yearly amounts. So I'll do the other calculation on this to get our coefficient of variation as well, just to round out our calculations here. And then we'll do our net present value calculation with the numbers that we had received. So let's take a look at these. We're going to say we have this equals the 300, the 800 and the 100. The expected value or average value is going to be then the 680 going to bring that all the way down, 680, it will subtract this out. This is going to be the 300 minus the 680. Going to copy that down. Put our cursor on that, use the fill handle to copy it down.

Squaring it. Now, this is going to be equal. This number squared shift, six carat, number two four square it. I'm doing this more rapidly. Note because we have seen this in prior problems. You can go back to the prior problems. You want to spend more time on these calculations. Just good practice to do it multiple times and then copy that down square routine, all of them. And then apply out our probabilities, which are the 40, 20, 40 this time, going to select these three cells and make them a percent, no group percentages in them copying the 40 control see down arrows holding down, shift down again, control V to paste, and then we'll multiply this out the 144 four times to 40 percent, the 14 four times the 20 percent. The one or two, four times the 40 percent underlying font group and underline summing it up equals DSU and shift nine up arrow holding down shift up and enter.

We got the one one six that's going to be our variance. So we got the variance. Let's do the standard deviation, which is the square root of that number. So we're going to say this is going to be equal to this or not like that. That's not how you do it. That's not how it works as a square root formula function, whatever that is, square root of that number. And then let's add some decimals. Numbers, a couple of decimals there, and then we have the expected value that we calculated, which was that average, the average we did over here, the six eight zero underlining that and go into the fight group and underline that's going to give us our coefficient of variation dividing this out. This is going to be equal to this, divided by this, and then I'm going to add some decimals there. So there we have that.

Let's do it for the second one. Just to practice this out. Practice's coefficient calculation. This equals 500. Copy that. Control C down control, holding down shift and control. The expected value is going to be eight thirty. This is going to be equal to the cell above it. I'm going to copy that. Control C down arrow control V. The difference is the five hundred minus the eight thirty. I'm going to copy that. Control C down arrow holding shift down again. Control the going to square it. This equals the negative three thirty shift six carat in other words two to the power of two. Copy in that control C down arrow holding down shift down arrow again control the probabilities.

That's going to be our thirty percent. I'm going to select these three cells, make them %s by going to the no group percentages in them. Copy the thirty control see down arrow holding shift down control v multiplying one zero eight nine times the thirty percent copy in that cell control see down arrow holding shift down arrow control v. Let's put an underlying here by go into the fight group and underline and then sum it up with the S you m sum it up with the S you and and that's going to be then the variance. Standard deviation, standard deviation is going to then be equal to the rescue square root q r t shift nine up arrow enter adding some decimals, no group a couple of decimals. Then we'll take the expected value, which I'm just going to say is equal to this name up there.

Expected value is the 830 underline on that one. Let's underline it, put the line underneath. No one has the underline; the line underneath is known as the underline and then we'll divide this out. The 272 twenty one divided by the eight thirty added some decimals. No couple of decimals. Let's do that one more time and then we'll get to the new thing here. So we'll just practice this one more time. Last one before hundred copies. Copy that. Copy that. Roger out. Copy that, Roger. And then we're going to say the expected value is six eighty. You're going to say this. This equals the 680 copy that pasted here. So there we have that. And then the difference, the four hundred minus the six eighty.

Copy that control c hold and shift down, control the square int it equals the negative to eighty shift six to to the power of two. Copy that control see down arrow holding shift down again. Control the probabilities. Let's select these three cells. Make them a percent no group percent to find them. This is going to be the forty forty. This is the forty copy that controls. See down shift down again. Control the multiplying out the seventy eight four times to forty percent. Copy that control see down arrow holding shift down down control the underline the line underneath. No one has the underline and then equals you and the sum shift nine. And there we have that. That's the coefficient of variation again.

So we've done that a few times now, it's probably nauseating, but that's good, it's a good nauseate and this is going to be this Scutari shift nine square root, no group adds in a couple decimals of expected value then the value that we expect. This is what we expect. Let me lay down my expectations here. Expectation 680. That's what's expected of you. Investment, and then we've got the coefficient of variation, which is going to be equal to the standard deviation divided by the expected value, and then we'll add some decimals. So there we have that. OK, so now it's finally the net present value, which is kind of like the new thing that we collect. We want to go to you here.

So we're going to do the net present value a little bit tricky because we have zero zero year one and then we skipped up to year three and then year five. I want to make sure I put the year's in here so that we could use these as a cell reference. I'm going to center this and then we just pick up our numbers. I'm going to say year one was the initial investment that went out. We're imagining the one thousand four hundred and I'm sorry, year zero. And then in year one is our expected value of the eight thirty eight six six eighty and then year two. And we had no, no, no return year three, we're going to imagine the return is eight thirty. And then we skipped up to year five. No return in year four. It's actually not year five, it's year nine. It should be six eighty. This should be a nine year nine.

So there we have it. And then if we have those properly allocated, we can use our present value calculation, picking up these numbers to the left. So in other words, the negative present value shift of nine rate is going to be equal to this 15 percent. I'm going to do this faster because we've seen these in the past EF four on the keyboard so I can copy it down comma, number of periods of zero this time, which means we're going to get the same result, but it'll allow us to copy it down, comma, comma. Future value is going to be that one thousand four and enter the same number because at period zero then I'm going to copy that and then paste the formula down and double click to see if it's doing what we think it should. It is.

Is it picking up the right rate? Let's use our little pointer thing over here, see if it's going to the right rate. You could find those, by the way, and it's the review area, the review. It notes the formulas area. These things have your pointer to show you what's going in that formula. There it is that fifteen is included in there somewhere. So I think that's good. I'm going to remove my pointer line and sum this up equals the assumed summing that up. Underline here font group and underline this is going to be the total or the net present value. Now note that the skipping around on the years might bother you. So let's build this table just having our normal kind of years here just to see what that would look like if I went zero one and then we brought this up to nine years to get a better idea.

And this might give a good idea if we were to present a project like this, which is a little bit weird in its nature, so that we can present a better understanding of what's happening from year to year. Right. We'd say, well, the initial investment went out, which was one thousand four. We're going to get a return after the first year of the six eighty and then zero return in year two and then year three, we're going to get a return of the eight thirty zero return for five, six, seven, eight. And then in year nine, we're going to get a return of about a negative return, a return of eight thirty. And that's an unusual structure. So we're just adding an unusual kind of return structure here. But that's what we're looking at.

So now we're going to say then the present value of that negative present value, same calculation shift nine rate is going to be that fifteen percent. And then let's say F for on the keyboard comma number a period zero, comma, comma, future value, same number here. I'm going to then copy that down. And so there we have it now, this last one. Year nine is wrong, year nine should be the 680. There we have it, so that's right, and then we can sum this up, this equals the sum. And so then we get to the same result and now you could see each of the years and that might be a better pictorial way to to think about it. If you were to display it to someone. Obviously, it's a little bit more work possible to do. Let's make it nice and pretty, put it blue.

Everybody likes the light blue and then we'll put some brackets around it. That looks excellent. Looks excellent. Let's put an underline here under the line. So just know this is another way that you could basically use this, this kind of analysis on this capital budgeting, long term decision making process. We had uneven payments and then we're thinking we can use this process to analyze what we believe the influence would be on a year to year basis. Possibly giving us a better or more accurate thought process in terms of the actual inflows that are going to happen on a year to year basis and then use our net present value once we have the expected values on a year to year type of basis.

www.ingramcontent.com/pod-product-compliance
Lightning Source LLC
Chambersburg PA
CBHW071917210526
45479CB00002B/454